P9-CAA-998

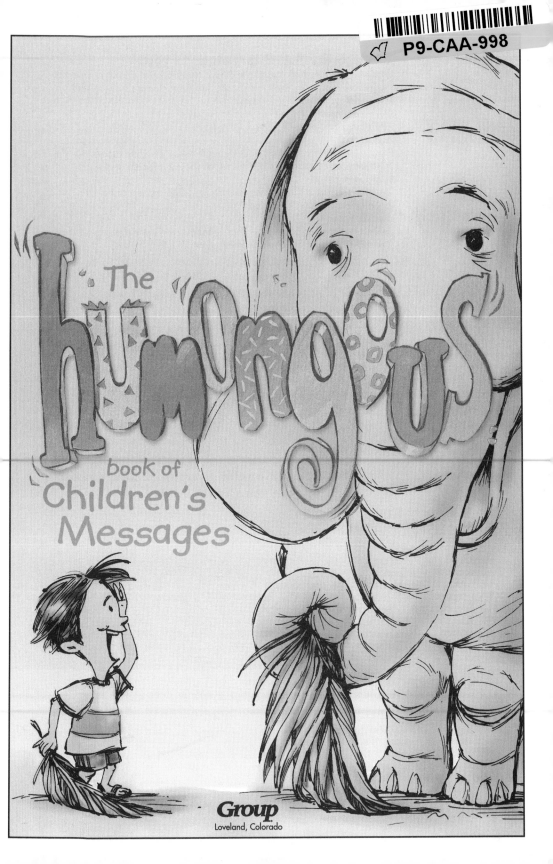

The humongous book of Children's Messages

Group
Loveland, Colorado

Group's R.E.A.L. Guarantee® to you:

This Group resource incorporates our R.E.A.L. approach to ministry—one that encourages long-term retention and life transformation. It's ministry that's:

Relational
Because learner-to-learner interaction enhances learning and builds Christian friendships.

Experiential
Because what learners experience through discussion and action sticks with them up to 9 times longer than what they simply hear or read.

Applicable
Because the aim of Christian education is to equip learners to be both hearers and doers of God's Word.

Learner-based
Because learners understand and retain more when the learning process takes into consideration how they learn best.

The Humongous Book of Children's Messages
Copyright © 2004 Group Publishing, Inc.

All rights reserved. No part of this book may be reproduced in any manner whatsoever without prior written permission from the publisher, except where noted in the text and in the case of brief quotations embodied in critical articles and reviews. For information, write Permissions, Group Publishing, Inc., Dept. PD, P.O. Box 481, Loveland, CO 80539.

Visit our Web site: **group.com**

Credits
Authors: Deaconess Kristen Baltrum, Gwyn D. Borcherding, Jody Brolsma, Teryl Cartwright, Rick Chromey, Susan Irons Crittenden, Heather A. Eades, Enelle G. Eder, Kylie Erickson, Nancy Wendland Feehrer, Donald Hinchey, Margaret Rickers Hinchey, Carmen Kamrath, Bob Latchaw, Christopher Perciante, Larry Shallenberger, Kathryn Hayes Sparks, Lee Sparks, Sharyn Spradlin, Bonnie Temple, Becki West, and Gordon D. West
Editors: Linda A. Anderson and Cindy S. Hansen
Creative Development Editor: Mikal Keefer
Chief Creative Officer: Joani Schultz
Copy Editor: Dena Twinem
Art Director: Randy Kady
Computer Graphic Artist: Lynn Gardner
Cover Art Director/Designer: Bambi Eitel
Cover Illustrators: Michael Morris and Lindy Burnett
Interior Illustrator: Michael Morris
Production Manager: Peggy Naylor

Unless otherwise noted, Scripture taken from the HOLY BIBLE, NEW INTERNATIONAL VERSION®. Copyright © 1973, 1978, 1984 by International Bible Society. Used by permission of Zondervan Publishing House. All rights reserved.

Library of Congress Cataloging-in-Publication Data
The humongous book of children's messages/[authors, Kristen Baltrum etal.].--1st American pbk.ed
     p. cm.
   ISBN 978-0-7644-2647-6 (pbk.)
   1. Children's sermons. I. Baltrum, Kristen.
   BV4315.H88 2004
   252'.53--dc22   2003017336
10 9 8   13 12 11 10 09 08

Printed in the United States of America.

The Humongous Book of Children's Messages

Group
Loveland, Colorado

Table of Contents

Messages for New Testament Stories

Messages for Topical Stories

Messages for Holiday Stories

Indexes

How to Use This Book

Presenting a children's message is *always* an adventure.

When Matt waves his little hand in the air to get your attention, is it because he's just discovered a Bible truth—or because he has to go to the bathroom? When you ask kids how they serve their parents, will Nancy talk about cleaning her room or picking up beer cans after Dad's card game last Friday night?

Children's messages are always an adventure...and they can always be fun, too.

Here are more than 170 children's messages contributed by people like you—people who stand in front of groups of children and tell them about God. You're getting their best messages, organized so it's easy for you to find just the right message for a children's sermon, a devotion, or to complement a Sunday school lesson.

Handy indexes make it a snap to find the perfect idea—fast. And here are some practical insights about how to deliver these messages in a way that gives you maximum impact...

Personalize messages.

If there's a story about shoveling snow and you live in Los Angeles, substitute a childhood activity from your own experience. Feel free to adapt these messages as you see fit.

Be careful about questions.

You want children involved, so asking questions is great—but what will you do when forty-seven hands shoot up and everyone wants to talk?

If possible, have children sit in small groups with adult leaders. That way, when you ask a question, children can tell leaders their answers while you wait. Then you can ask several leaders to share stories that came out of their groups' discussions. That way, more children get to talk, and what's shared publicly has been filtered through an adult.

Affirm all contributors—no matter what.

You ask who died on the cross, and Jasmine confidently blurts out, "The Easter Bunny!" (Don't laugh—it's happened.) Be sure to affirm Jasmine for answering even as you get back on track and talk about Jesus.

Position kids so they're focused on you.

If you present a children's message in "Big People's Church" by calling kids up to the front of the room, seat children so they're focused on you and aren't distracted by the audience in the pews.

And a word about Big People: If they're parents of children, they'll be praying their kids don't do or say anything embarrassing.

If the adults *aren't* parents, they'll be equally attentive but for a different reason: They're praying the children *do* find a way to do or say something embarrassing. Those adults can't wait for some wide-eyed, innocent preschooler to hand you a hot potato.

Use props visible from the back pew.

If you use a prop in a message, make sure everyone can see it—including adults who may be watching from a distance. Children want to see what you're holding, so find a way to make it visible.

Have fun.

You're sharing truths from God's Word. You're getting to hang out with people who love playing. It's a great combination! Enjoy your time with kids!

Allergy Alert

You'll see this icon throughout the book wherever food is used. Be aware that some children have food allergies that can be dangerous. Know your children, and consult with parents about allergies their children may have. Also be sure to carefully read food labels, as hidden ingredients may cause allergy-related problems.

Messages for Old Testament Stories

God Made the World

Topic: Creation

Scripture: Genesis 1:1–31

Simple Supplies: You'll need a Bible, a globe, a flashlight, a larger light such as a lamp, and a black tarp. Set the globe on a table with the lights underneath. Cover the whole thing in black tarp.

Open your Bible to Genesis 1, and show the kids the words.

LEADER

Depending on the size of your group, vary the number of children you position throughout the story. If you have a large group, use more children to be trees and animals. If you have fewer children, use them to play all the roles.

Say: **Today we're going to talk about God making the world. Look at this black tarp. Before God made the world, there was only darkness. Everyone close your eyes to make it dark. Now cover your eyes with your hands so it's even darker. That's what God created everything out of!** Take the tarp off the globe and have children open their eyes. **I'll tell you the things God made each day when he was creating our world. After each one, you say, "And God saw it was good."** Have kids repeat the phrase.

On the first day, God made light and he separated the light from the darkness. Have kids open and shut their eyes several times. **He called the light "day" and the darkness "night"! And God saw it was good.** Have kids repeat the phrase.

On the second day, God made the sky. Everyone put your hands on top of your eyes as if you're looking up high into the sky. And God saw it was good. Have kids repeat the phrase.

On the third day, God made the land, trees, and plants. Position a few children by the globe, and have them spread their arms like branches. Have the children tell you what kind of tree or plant they would like to be. **And God saw it was good.** Have kids repeat the phrase.

On the fourth day, God made the sun (shine the large light onto the globe, and let someone hold it)**, the moon** (shine the flashlight onto the globe, and let someone hold it)**, and the stars!** Place a couple of children by the globe, and have them open and close their hands like twinkling stars. **And God saw it was good.** Have kids repeat the phrase.

On the fifth day, God made the fish and birds. Ask one child to move his or her hands like a swimming fish and another child to flap his or her arms like wings. Ask them what kind of fish or bird they would like to be. **And God saw it was good.** Have kids repeat the phrase.

On the sixth day, God made people and animals. Choose one child to be Adam, and have the rest be any kind of animal they want. Have them tell you what kind of animal they would like to be. **And God saw it was good.** Have kids repeat the phrase.

On the seventh day, God rested! Have everyone wipe the sweat off their brows, take a deep breath, and sit down. **God saw all that he had made, and God saw that it was good!** Have the kids repeat the phrase.

Shut off the two lights, gather the children, and ask:

- **Of all the things God created, what do you like most?**
- **How can we thank God for creating so many wonderful things?**

Say: **I love all of God's creation, don't you? We can thank God for his creation by praying to him, by singing to him, and by taking care of the world and all that's in it. Let's thank God for all the things he created. I'll begin, and then you can name anything in God's creation you are thankful for. Dear God, we thank you for the world you created, especially...**(pause for kids to share). **In Jesus' name, amen.**

 One teacher told a group of children, "Today we're going to talk about when God created everything. It's in our Bibles in Genesis 1:1." Four-year-old Caleb quickly replied, "No, Teacher, that's Genesis 9-1-1!"

God Made People

Topic: Names

Scripture: Genesis 1:26–31; 2:4–25

Simple Supplies: You'll need a Bible, marker, and name tags (two per child). Write "Child of God" on each name tag.

Say: **I was walking into the blossom today, and I saw the marshmallow talking to one of the golf shoes. The marshmallow wanted a score-board for the hand cream so they could learn about the chicken hawks. Anyway, after I saw them I walked in here to the snorkel and saw all of you bluebottles sitting here, so I thought I'd deliver a blue-bottle cranberry. And that's why I'm here.** Look at the children's confused expressions, then ask:

> **LEADER TIP**
>
> If you have a book of names and their meanings, bring it to the message time. Look up the meanings of several children's names.

• **What's wrong? Didn't you understand me? Why not?**

Say: **Things we talk about all have names, don't they? We know what things are called, and it helps us talk to each other about the world around us.** Open your Bible to Genesis 2. **Did you ever wonder how things got their names? We know how all the animals got their names. The Bible tells us that God brought the animals to Adam to see what he would name them. He got to give a name to every living creature!**

All of you are named as well. Your parents gave you your names. Sometimes parents name their children after other people in the family, after songs, after people in movies, or because they want a name that means something very special. One family had six kids and then had another little girl. They named her Amanda, which means "much loved," because she had so many brothers and sisters to love her. Ask the children if they know how they got their names. **Here are what some other names**

mean. *Amy* means "beloved" and *Dakota* means "friend." In Australia the pretty name *Kylie* means "boomerang," and in Greece the name *Theodore* means "gift of God." *Diana* means "heavenly" and *Walter* means "ruler of the army." Ask:

- **Do any of you know the meaning of your name?** Allow kids to respond. If you brought a name book, read some meanings from it.

Say: **It's fun to know names and meanings. It helps us look at ourselves in a new way! I think Adam must have looked at creation in a new way once he named everything. The neat thing is, no matter what your name is, no matter what it means, we all have another special name, and that's "Child of God." God made creation, and God made you. You are a child of God.**

Give each child a name tag to wear. As you do, pray: **Dear God, thanks for all the names of all of your creation. Thanks especially for naming** [name of child] **"Child of God."** Continue thanking God for each child as you place a name tag on each one. **In Jesus' name, amen.** Once every child is wearing a name tag, give each one a second name tag. **Give this second name tag away so someone else knows he or she is also named "Child of God."**

Adam and Eve Sin

Topic: Temptation

Scripture: Genesis 3:1-24

Simple Supplies: You'll need a Bible, a bowl of M&Ms candies, and a sign that says, "Don't eat. Save for tonight's party." Bring packets of candy or fruit chews (one packet per child).

Hold the bowl of M&Ms, and show kids the sign. Say: **Today we're going to hear a familiar story from the Bible. But first, let's read**

this sign on this bowl of yummy candy: **"Don't eat. Save for tonight's party." OK, hmmm. I guess we won't eat any candy. We can just look at it while I tell you the story.** Open your Bible to Genesis 3, and show the kids the words. **Anyway, the story is about the first two people in the world—Adam and Eve. They lived in the lovely Garden of Eden. God cared for Adam and Eve and gave them all that he created for them to enjoy.** "Absent-mindedly" reach into the bowl, get a candy, and then eat it. **In the middle of the garden there was one tree they weren't supposed to touch. God told them not to eat its fruit. Also in the garden with Adam and Eve was a serpent—that's a kind of snake.** Eat another candy. **The Bible tells us that the serpent was "crafty" or sneaky. And he talked the woman into eating the fruit.** Eat a candy. **Uh-oh! That was wrong. Then Adam ate some fruit. Uh-oh! That was wrong!** Eat a candy. **When Adam and Eve ate the fruit, everything changed for them. They knew they had done wrong. So they hid from God.** Eat a candy. Ask:

- **How did Adam and Eve disobey God?**
- **When do we disobey and break rules in our lives?**

While the kids answer, continue to eat candies. If a child points out that you're eating the candy, pause. If no child points it out, pretend that someone noticed and shrug. Say: **Looks like I've been breaking this rule. But the candies are so good, and there's so many—it's not a problem, is it?** Let children respond. **The rule was "Don't eat this candy," so it really isn't right for me to eat it, is it? Just because we're tempted, it's not right for us to break a rule. Because they broke God's rule, Adam and Eve had to leave the garden. But God still loved them and cared for them. Even though we disobey God, he'll forgive us when we ask. God loves us and cares for us, just as he loved and continued to care for Adam and Eve.**

Ask the children to close their eyes for a prayer. Pray: **Dear God, please forgive us when we disobey. Thank you for continuing to love us, care for us, and give us great gifts. In Jesus' name, amen.** When kids open their eyes, surprise them with the snacks and let them each have one.

Noah Builds the Ark

Topic: God's Care

Scripture: Genesis 6:5-22

Simple Supplies: You'll need a Bible and fifteen to twenty chairs (enough so when the chairs are in a circle, the group of kids can sit inside).

Open your Bible to Genesis 6:5-22. Say: **Today's story is about an ark, which is a big, big boat. Many years after God made Adam and Eve, the people on earth began to forget about God and chose not to follow God's ways. They became evil and did many bad things. God was sad that the people on earth had sinned against him so much. There was only one man left who was good. The Bible said he "walked with God." His name was Noah! That's amazing that he chose to follow God's ways when everyone else did not! Let's hear it for Noah!** Lead the kids in a cheer. **God told Noah he was sad he made the world and that he was going to send a flood to destroy it. But God told Noah he was going to keep Noah and his family and the animals safe. God wanted Noah and his family to build a big ark to put a lot of animals on, and he told Noah exactly how he wanted the ark to be built.**

Let's pretend we are Noah and his family building the ark. The chairs are our ark-building materials. Let's make the ark big, because we'll be filling it with lots of animals. We have to be sure to leave a door for the animals to enter. Guide the kids in arranging the chairs into an ark shape. Leave one chair out of the ark shape to be a doorway.

Once it's "built," gather kids outside. Tell the children to pretend to be animals. They can choose to be any animal such as a bird, cow, or kangaroo. Have them move and make noise like the animals they have chosen to be. Stand in the middle and motion with your hand for the children to come into the "ark." Say: **Come on board!** When all the "animals" are inside the ark, say: **The Bible tells us that God cared** for Noah, his family, and the animals. God himself shut the door to keep them safe. Pull the remaining chair into the opening so all the animals are "safe" inside. Ask:

- **How did God care for Noah and the animals?**
- **How does God care for us?**

Say: **God cared for Noah by telling him ahead of time to build an ark. God told Noah how to build it so it would be a home for lots of animals when the flood came. God cares for us, too, by giving us food, families, homes, and our wonderful church. Let's thank God for the way he cares for us.**

Pray: **Dear God thank you for caring for Noah and the animals, and thank you for caring for me.**

Let kids out of the ark one by one, and have them say, "Thanks for your care, God" as they exit.

The Animals Climb Aboard

Topic: God's Protection

Scripture: Genesis 7:1-16

Simple Supplies: You'll need a Bible, stuffed animals, and a large basket.

LEADER TIP

If you can find small animal toys, such as Beanie Babies plush toys, you will be able to get more animals in the basket to hand out to the children.

Open your Bible to Genesis 7:1-16, and show the children the words. Say: **Today we're going to talk about Noah, who built a large boat called an ark. The ark was huge—even bigger than this room. God told Noah that there was going to be a big rainstorm. The rainstorm would cause a huge flood. The flood would cover everything on the whole earth! But God wanted** to protect the animals, so he told Noah to get ready for two of all the animals to come on the ark. Let's look in my basket and see if we can find some animals. Give a stuffed animal to each child. **Now we're going to have an animal parade. Everyone find a partner, and follow me around the room.** Help the children line up two by two then follow you around the room and back again. Encourage the kids to each move and make noises like the animal he or she has.

LEADER

If you have musicians in the room, have them play "Rise and Shine (The Arky, Arky Song)" to accompany the parade, or play another upbeat familiar marching song. You could also have a sound person play a recording of this song.

Gather the children in front, then say: **Can you imagine what that must have been like to see all those animals coming onto the boat? They probably lined up for miles to get on board the ark with Noah.** Ask:

- **How did God protect the animals?**
- **How does God protect us?**

Say: **God protected the animals by getting them on board the ark so Noah and his family could care for them. God protects us by giving us food, homes, friends, and families who love us. When bad things happen in the world, God tells us to trust him to take care of us. Next time you go to bed and see your favorite stuffed animal, remember that just like God cared for the animals on the ark, God cares for you.**

Ask the kids to place the animals back in the basket, and as they do, pray: **Dear God, thank you for loving and protecting** [child's name]. Continue praying for each child as each one places the stuffed animal in the basket. **In Jesus' name, amen.**

 A pastor was giving a children's message about Noah and the animals. Here's how it went:

Pastor: What did God ask Noah to do?
Child: Build an ark!
Pastor: And then what did God ask Noah to do?
Child: Get two of each kind of animal.
Pastor: And what was Noah supposed to do with the animals?
Child: Put them on a cross?
Pastor: No...that comes a little later in the story.

The Boat Begins to Float (1)

Topic: Facing Fears

Scripture: Genesis 7:17–8:3

Simple Supplies: You'll need a Bible, a large clear fishbowl or bowl of water, and a toy boat to place on top of the water. Ask a musician on piano or drums to make loud stormlike noises during the message, beginning with a loud thunder-type noise and then adding rain sounds. The rain should be gentle at first, but then build, including more thunder.

Say: **Hello everyone!** The musician should hit the drums or piano loudly to make the sound of thunder. Put your hands over your ears like you are ducking. **Wow! That sounded like thunder to me! Does it look like it's going to rain?** Look up. Ask:

- **How many of you have been in a scary thunderstorm?**
- **What was it like?**
- **What did you feel during the storm?**

Open your Bible to Genesis 7:17, and show the children the words. Say: **We might get soaked if we're caught in a rainstorm. Sometimes the thunder and lightning can be scary, even if we're inside. Today's Bible story is about Noah, his family, and the animals that were in the ark.** Ask kids to tell you what they remember about that story. **Yes, God sent rain and Noah's ark began to float! It rained for forty days and forty nights. That's a long, long time. Let's pretend we're in the storm with them.** Hold the bowl of water with the toy boat in it so kids can see. Have the musician start with gentle sounds, then get louder and louder. **I hear the rain starting.** Sway back and forth. Encourage the kids to move too. **The thunder is getting louder. It's getting closer!** Sway back and forth, making the water in the bowl sway back and forth as well. **Oh my, the storm is really coming.** Duck each time you hear the thunder. **I think it's been about forty days and forty nights now! I think the storm is fading.** The musician should play softer until the storm dies out. **Well,**

look at this. Hold the bowl so kids can see. **Through the whole storm, my little boat stayed afloat, and I'm sure the people and animals inside didn't even get wet. God protected Noah's family and the animals throughout the storm.** Ask:

LEADER

For added drama, recruit volunteers to spray a mist of water on the children and flash the lights on and off.

- **How do you think Noah's family and the animals felt during the rain?**
- **What tough times do you sometimes face?**

Say: **Noah and his family must have been afraid in the storm, but God protected them and kept them safe. We might feel afraid if we have to move to a new place or go to a new school. But we can always trust God to help us when we're afraid.**

Ask a volunteer to pray for the situations mentioned during the questions. Give the person the boat and bowl of water to hold as he or she prays. Close by praying: **Dear God, thank you that you are with us when we go through hard times. Help us remember you are there. In Jesus' name, amen.**

The Boat Begins to Float (2)

Topic: Patience

Scripture: Genesis 7:17–8:12

Simple Supplies: You'll need a Bible.

Gather the children around you. Ask:

- **Who has ever gone on a long trip in the car?**
- **Have you ever asked your parents, "Are we there yet?"**

Say: **Sometimes it's hard to wait when all we want to do is get out and stretch our legs. We need to have patience during a long**

trip. Open your Bible to Genesis 7, and show the children the words. **Noah and his family and the animals were riding on the ark for a long time. Maybe some of Noah's family asked him, "Are we there yet?"**

Tell the children the following facts, and lead them in counting out loud as indicated.

- **Noah and his family and all those animals had to wait inside the ark for forty days while the storm raged, the winds blew, the rain fell, and the earth was covered with water. Let's count to forty.** Start counting to forty. **One, two, three, four, five...wait a minute, it would take too long to count to forty that way. Let's count by tens. Ten, twenty, thirty, forty! Forty days! I bet they were ready to get out of that boat! "Are we there yet?" "No!"**
- **Noah and his family and all those animals had to wait 150 days for the water to go down just enough for the ark to barely touch the top of a mountain. Everyone count to 150. One, two, three, four, five...wait a minute, it would take too long to count to 150 that way. Let's count by fifties: 50, 100, 150. One hundred and fifty days! "Are we there yet?" "No!"**
- **They waited two and a half more months for the water to go down enough so that the ark stopped on the top of a mountain. That's almost all of summer vacation from school—about seventy-five days. Let's count to seventy-five. One, two, three, four, five...wait a minute, it would take too long to count to seventy-five that way. Let's count by fives: 5, 10, 15, 20, 25, 30, 35, 40, 45, 50, 55, 60, 65, 70, 75. Seventy-five days! "Are we there yet?" "No!"**
- **All those smelly animals in one boat, but Noah waited forty more days before he even opened the window for the first time. Let's count by twos: 2, 4, 6, 8, 10, 12, 14, 16, 18, 20, 22, 24, 26, 28, 30, 32, 34, 36, 38, 40. Forty days! Noah opened the window and sent a dove out to see if he could find dry land, but the dove came back. "Are we there yet?" "No!"**
- **After seven more days, Noah sent out the dove again, and it came back with an olive branch. Let's count to seven: 1, 2, 3, 4, 5, 6, 7. Seven days! "Are we there yet?" "Almost!"**
- **Finally, after seven *more* days, Noah sent out the dove, and it didn't come back. Count the last seven days: 1, 2, 3, 4, 5, 6, 7!**

All those days we counted were almost one whole year for the ark to finally get to the end of its trip. Noah, his family, and all of those animals had to have a lot of patience to trust that God knew what he was doing and would bring them back to dry

land. **The next time you go on a long trip, remember Noah, and have patience!**

Have the children stand and pray: **Dear God, thank you for helping Noah to be patient on his long trip. Please help us have patience too. In Jesus' name, amen.** Have the children line up, and count them as they leave. As you say each number, have the children say, "Help me be patient."

Noah and the Rainbow (1)

Topics: Facing Fears, God Keeps His Promises

Scripture: Genesis 9:8-17

Simple Supplies: You'll need a Bible, tape, and twelve sheets of poster board (six black and six different bright colors). Tape each black sheet of poster board to a colorful sheet back to back, so you have six sheets.

Open your Bible to Genesis 9, and show the kids the words.

Say: **Today's Bible story is about Noah and the rainbow. It's the happy ending to the story of the flood. Yea! I love happy endings. Noah and his family and all those animals were riding on an ark, so they were kept safe from the floodwaters.** Ask:

- **What might Noah and his family have feared during the flood and the long time they were on the ark?**
- **What fears do you have today?**

Hand out the six sheets of poster board, and have six kids hold them so the black side is facing out. Ask them to stand in a line, facing the audience, so the audience can see the dark poster board. Say: **Noah and his family might have been afraid the flood would never end, or that they'd run out of food for the animals.** Mention other ideas the kids said. **We might have fears like "I'm afraid to go to my first sleepover," or "I'm afraid of mean people."** Mention other ideas kids said. **We all face dark moments like these. Our fears are like these dark posters here.** Point to the children holding the dark poster board.

God promised to take care of Noah, his family, and the animals. And we know that God always keeps his promises! God fed Noah and the animals, God kept them safe and dry, and God dried up the earth and let the ark land. Ask:

- **How did God care for Noah?**
- **How does God care for us?**

As you talk about God's love and care and repeat kids' answers, have the poster holders turn their posters over so the bright colors show. Then position them into an arc-shaped rainbow. If you have stairs, have kids stand on the different levels. Or, you could position kids two standing, two kneeling, and two sitting. Say: **Noah knew God had kept his promise to keep them safe, because God set a rainbow in the sky as a reminder! When we turn our fears over to God, he can show us the brightness of his love for us, just like the bright colors of the rainbow.**

Have the children who do not have a piece of poster board stand around the "rainbow" as you pray: **Dear God, thank you for the bright colors of the rainbow. Each time we see one of these colors, help us to remember that you are with us and will help us when we are afraid. In Jesus' name, amen.** Have each of the children holding the poster board hand it to you as they leave.

Noah and the Rainbow (2)

Topic: God Keeps His Promises

Scripture: Genesis 9:8-17

Simple Supplies: You'll need a Bible and washable markers.

Say: **Who here knows who Noah was?** Pause for children to answer. **Right. God told Noah that he would send a flood. He wanted Noah to build a big boat so that his family and the animals would be safe. The story of Noah is one of hope and promise.** Open your Bible to Genesis 9:8-17, and show the children the words. **The Bible says that God protected Noah's family and the animals during the flood. After it was all over, God put a sign in the sky—a rainbow!**

Rainbows are some of the prettiest and happiest signs we have. They come after a rainstorm. God told Noah that he put the rainbow in the sky as a reminder that God keeps his promises.

Sometimes we need reminders like the rainbow. So today I brought some washable markers. Hand a marker to each child. **Maybe you know someone who uses a Palm Pilot, which is a mini computer, to remind them of things. Today, we are going to make our own palm reminder. Take your washable marker and draw a rainbow on the palm of your hand. First draw one curved line, then trade markers with someone and put another color below it. Three colors are enough.** While kids do this, discuss:

- **What does the rainbow remind us of?**
- **Why is it important to keep your promises?**
- **How do you feel knowing God keeps his promises?**

Say: **The rainbow reminds us that God cared for and loved Noah's family and the animals, and God cares for and loves us, too! God always keeps his promises!**

Collect the markers, and ask the kids to look at their palm rainbow reminders as you pray: **Thank you, God, for loving us and for**

keeping your promises. In Jesus' name, amen. As the children leave or go back to their seats, have them hold up their palm reminders and wave!

The People Build a Tall Tower (1)

Topic: Pride

Scripture: Genesis 11:1-9

Simple Supplies: You'll need a Bible.

LEADER TIP

You could gather a bag of sports equipment for this children's message. Gather a baseball cap for each child, and several balls and baseball mitts. Hand out the equipment as the children come forward for the message.

Say: **OK guys, let's pretend I'm your coach and you're my team. We're going to be a really great team. We're going to be famous! I am so excited! I want everyone to know about us. In fact, I want the whole world to know about our team. Go! Go! Go!** Ask:

• **What kinds of things do we need to be a great team?**

As the children mention things, act out some of them. For "exercise," lead them in doing jumping jacks. For "practice," have them pretend to toss and catch balls. At the end, lead them in a cheer. Say: **Two! Four! Six! Eight! Who do we appreciate? Us! Us! Us!**

I am so excited about our team. I want the world to know about us! We're going to be famous! Hey, wait a minute. Before we really get serious about our fame, let's stop and hear a Bible story for today.

Ask the team to sit as you open your Bible to Genesis 11:1-9. Say: **Our Bible story is about people who wanted to build a tall tower. Building a tall tower isn't a bad thing in itself. What *was* bad was that the people were doing it to be famous. They wanted to do it to make their own name great. Not once did the people mention God! They had taken their eyes off of God. He wasn't number one in their lives anymore.**

We were having fun pretending to be a great team. Being a great team and being famous *isn't bad* if we keep our eyes on God and use our fame to tell the world about our wonderful God.

But the people in our story didn't keep focused on God. God wanted them to do that, so he came up with a creative solution. Here's what he did.

Goo goo blah blah na na na na na goo goo blah blah na na na na goo goo blah blah na na na na goo goo blah blah na na na na. All the while you are babbling, try to "coach" your team. Watch the confused looks! Ask:

- **What would happen to a team if they couldn't understand their coach?**

Say: **There would be confusion! They couldn't work together! God made the people building the tower speak different languages. They couldn't keep working on their "let's be famous" project. They had to go out and do other things. God wants us to keep our eyes on him and honor him only! Let's ask for his help in doing that.**

Pray: **Dear God, help us not be like the people building the tower. Help up to keep our focus on you and use any fame we have to tell others about you.** Then lead kids in cheering: **Two! Four! Six! Eight! Who do we appreciate? God! God! God!**

The People Build a Tall Tower (2)

Topic: God Is Number One

Scripture: Genesis 11:1-9

Simple Supplies: You'll need a Bible, table, and large blocks. Place the blocks on the floor by the table.

Open your Bible to Genesis 11:1-9, and show the children the words. Say: **The Bible tells us about some people who wanted to be important and make a name for themselves. They wanted to be famous! So the people decided to build a tower up to heaven. Let's try to build a tower too. Everyone take a block, and we'll start here on the floor.** Begin on the floor, and put all the blocks on top of each other. Then stand back and look at it.

Hmm! What do you think? Do you think everyone here can see our tower? Can we build our tower taller? We want everyone to see it so people will think we're cool builders. Carefully knock down the tower, and have kids take another block. This time, have them build a tower on top of the table. Then stand back and look at it. Ask:

- **Why might people want to build a tower that would reach the heavens?**
- **How do people try to make themselves important today?**

Say: **The people in the story wanted to build a tall tower so they would be famous. Everyone would see the tower and think, "Ooh. What cool builders." But God wants everyone to put him first. God wants us to tell others about him, not about how cool we are.** Knock down the tower. **God stopped the people from building. He made them speak in different languages so they would scatter across the earth. Kind of like our**

LEADER

If time allows, use a marker and write a number one on each block. Give a block to each child as a reminder to keep God number one.

blocks scattered on the floor. God wants us to place him first in our lives and tell others about him. God is number one!

Have each child pick up a block and hand it to you as you pray.

Dear God, thank you for reminding us how important you are. Help us to remember to keep you the most important thing in our lives. In Jesus' name, amen.

God Blesses Abram (1)

Topic: Blessings

Scripture: Genesis 12:1-8

Simple Supplies: You'll need a Bible, a bowl with a few pieces of candy or packs of fruit chews, and a large bag of candy or packs of fruit chews containing enough so each child can have two pieces or packs.

Open your Bible to Genesis 12:1-8, and show kids the words. Say: **The Bible tells us that God told a man named Abram to leave his country and go to a new place that God would show him. God said he would bless Abram if he did this. God said he would make Abram a great nation and lots of people would be blessed because of him. Let me show you an example of what this blessing thing looks like.**

Ask a child to take the bowl of candy and go around and give a piece to each child. Each time the child gives away a piece of candy, pour several more pieces into the bowl. Keep doing this until the child has given several pieces away and you have filled the bowl until it overflows. Ask:

- **What did I want the helper to do?**
- **What happened because the helper obeyed?**
- **What did God want Abram to do?**
- **What did God say he'd do for Abram?**

Say: **Because** [name of child] **did what I asked and gave away candy,** [name of child] **was blessed with even more candy. In fact, the bowl overflowed! When we bless others and obey God, God always blesses us back—to overflowing!**

Make sure each child has a treat. Have enough treats available so kids can each have one more. As they receive another treat, have them pray, "Thanks, God, for blessing me so much." Close with everyone saying, "In Jesus' name, amen."

God Blesses Abram (2)

Topic: God Guides Us

Scripture: Genesis 12:1-8

Simple Supplies: You'll need a Bible, a road map, and a large blank sheet of paper folded to look like a road map.

Gather the children, and ask:

- **How many of you have ever taken a road trip with your family?**
- **Where did you go?**
- **Did anyone use a road map? Why?**

Pull out the road map, and show it to the kids. Unfold the map, and point to a few sites. Say: **We use a road map to show us the direction we're supposed to go. It tells us if we need to take a different road, and it tells us how far we need to go until we reach our destination.**

Open your Bible to Genesis 12:1-8, then say: **In this Bible story, God talked to a man named Abram about his future. God told Abram to leave his homeland, his friends, and his parents. God told him to take his wife and just what they could carry and go to another land. Here's a map that Abram might have used when God gave him these instructions.** Unfold the large blank sheet of paper. **Hmmm. What's wrong with this map?** Pause for kids to share. **There's nothing on this map! In fact, Abram didn't have any map at all. He didn't know where he was going. All Abram knew was that God told him to go, and that's what he did. Wow! What faith!** Ask:

- **When have you had to follow some hard instructions?**
- **How did God help you?**

Say: **Maybe a gym teacher instructed you to climb that long rope that goes all the way to the ceiling. Maybe you doubted you could do it. The next time you have trouble following instructions or don't know whether to trust someone, ask God for faith. Ask God to guide you in the right way.**

Close with this prayer. **God, please hear us as we tell you some tough things we need to do.** Pause. **Please guide us and help us have faith that you will show us the way. In Jesus' name, amen.**

Abram's Faith

Topic: Faith

Scripture: Genesis 12; Hebrews 11:1

Simple Supplies: You'll need a Bible and a helium-filled balloon with a string tied to it.

Hold the string so the balloon is floating high. Ask:

- **Who knows what makes this balloon float high?**
- **How do you know the helium is there? Can you see it?**

Bring the balloon down, then let it float up high again. Say: **Even though we can't see it, we know the balloon has helium in it. The helium makes the balloon float high.**

Open your Bible to Hebrews 11:1, and read: **"Now faith is being sure of what we hope for and certain of what we do not see."**

Turn to Genesis 12, and show the children the words. Say: **The Bible tells us about a man named Abram who had that kind of faith. When told to go to a new land, he went! Abram didn't even know where he was going, but he had faith in God to lead him. Even though Abram couldn't see God, he knew God was real. Abram had faith in God and was blessed for his faith.** Ask:

- **Why do you think Abram had faith in God?**
- **How do we show others our faith in God?**

Say: **Abram trusted in God to lead him even though he couldn't see him. Even though we can't see God, we know he's real. We show our faith by treating others kindly, by telling others about Jesus, and by following God's Word—the Bible.**

Bring the balloon down and hold it. Say: **As we pray I want you to imitate what I do with this balloon. Right now crouch down low, and when I let the balloon fly up high, stand and stretch up high.**

Pray: **Dear God, even though we can't see you, we have faith and trust that you are real.** Let the balloon float high. **Thanks for Abram who trusted you and had faith in you too. Help our faith to grow and grow. In Jesus' name, amen.**

LEADER TIP

If your church has a helium tank, bring it to the children's sermon as well. You can let off a bit of the helium so kids hear something coming out of the tank but they can't see it. You can purchase inexpensive small helium tanks and balloons at discount stores.

Isaac Is Coming (1)

Topics: Faith, Joy

Scripture: Genesis 18:1-19; 21:1-7

Simple Supplies: You'll need a Bible and Snickers candy bars.

Ask:

- **When do we laugh?**
- **Why do we laugh?**
- **Who thinks they have a great laugh?**

Say: **I have a Snickers candy bar here for the winner. Does anyone know what a snicker is? Yes, it is a small kind of laugh.**

Have a laughing contest with several of the children who said they have a great laugh. Line the kids up front, and make your arms the laughometer (see the illustration below). Have the first volunteer laugh into a microphone. Ask the audience to applaud the laugher. Raise the laughometer according to the loudness of the applause. Go to the next volunteer and do the same thing. Raise the laughometer to the same height. Be sure to raise to the same height for each laugher.

After all the volunteers have laughed into the microphone, say that all the laughers are winners. Give each contestant a Snickers candy bar.

Open your Bible to Genesis 18, and show the children the words. Say: **In our Bible story, we hear of an old woman named Sarah. She laughed twice in the story. Once when she was told she would have a baby in her old age. She laughed because she thought it was too good to be true! The second time Sarah laughed was when it really happened. She had a baby when she was old.**

Pray: **Dear God, thank you for the surprises you give us in life. Help us enjoy each day and all of the many blessings you give us. In Jesus' name, amen.** Ask all the children to give one belly-busting bunch of laughter to end the message.

Isaac Is Coming (2)

Topic: Trust God

Scripture: Genesis 18:1-19; 21:1-7

Simple Supplies: Select three people with strong laughs—an adult, a teenager, and an older woman. Cue them ahead of time on what you'll have them do during the message. You'll also need a smiley face self-inking stamp.

LEADER

If you don't have a self-inking stamp to use on the children's hands, bring in a washable marker, and draw smiley faces on their hands.

Say: **Today we're going to talk about some things that may seem impossible to us. Sometimes there are things in our lives that seem so unbelievable that people laugh when they hear them.** [Name of adult]**, will you please stand up?** Pause. **What would you say if I told you that I was going to give you ten million dollars?** Wait for the adult to laugh loudly and the rest in the room to join in. [Name of teenager]**, will you please stand up?** Pause. **What would you say if I told you that you were someday going to be the leader of our country?** Wait for the teenager to laugh loudly and the rest in the room to join in. [Name of older woman]**, will you please stand up?** Pause. **What would you say if I told you that you were going to have a baby?** Wait for the older woman to laugh loudly and the rest in the room to join in. Ask:

- **Why do you think those people laughed when I asked them those questions?**

Say: **Yes, I think those three didn't believe what I told them. Most of us know that usually only younger women have babies. That's the way our bodies are made.** Open your Bible to Genesis 18, and show the children the words. **God told Sarah, who was older than most of your grandmothers, that she was going to have a baby. She thought she was way too old to have a baby, so she laughed. But in a short while, she did have a baby! Some** things may sound unbelievable to us, but God can do all things! Trust him!

After our prayer, I would like you to whisper something to me that you need to trust God about. I will put a smiley face on your hand to help you remember to trust God because he can do all things!

Have the children prepare for prayer by folding their hands and closing their eyes. Pray: **Dear God, I am so amazed at how truly powerful you are. You truly can do anything, like give an old woman named Sarah a baby. Help us to trust you and watch to see the powerful ways you work. In Jesus' name, amen.**

As the children leave, have them quickly whisper what they need to trust God for, and place smiley faces on their hands. If you have a large number of children, ask one or more adults to help you listen to the children and put smiley faces on their hands.

A Wife Is Found for Isaac

Topic: Prayer

Scripture: Genesis 24

Simple Supplies: You'll need a Bible and enough small, plain drinking cups for each child to have one. Give the Bible to an adult in the room, and ask that adult to hand your Bible to you *before* you finish praying. See the following directions.

Say: **Hey, everyone! I have a great Bible story to tell you. It's about a servant who was helping to find a wife for a man named Isaac. This servant did a lot of praying because he trusted God to answer his prayers and guide him. Hmm. Before I can finish my story, I need to look at my Bible, but I can't seem to find it. I'm going to pray that God helps me and guides me to my Bible.**

Dear God, thank you for the Bible that teaches us so much about you and how you love us. Please help me find my Bible so I can tell everyone the story for today. Have the volunteer bring your Bible to you. Thank the volunteer, then finish the prayer. **Thank you, God, that you always answer prayer. Thank you that you know what we need even before we pray it. In Jesus' name, amen.**

Open the Bible to Genesis 24, and show the children the words. Say: **Our Bible story says that the servant had been sent out by Isaac's father to find the right woman for Isaac to marry. He was praying for God's help. He had stopped by a well after many days of travel. There were women coming to that well to get water. The servant prayed that the woman who offered to water his camels would be the one to be Isaac's wife. Verse 15 says that "before he had finished praying," Rebekah came to him and offered water to him and for his camels. God knew what the servant needed and answered his prayer before he even finished praying! These cups will help remind you of the way Rebekah offered water to the servants and his camels. That was a powerful answer to the servant's prayer.** Give each child a paper cup. Ask:

- **How did I find the Bible for our story?**
- **How did the servant find a wife for Isaac?**

Say: **I arranged ahead of time for our volunteer to give me the Bible before I finished praying. I wanted to show you an example of how God answered the servant's prayer in the Bible. God knows our needs even before we pray about them. God wants us to pray, because it's how we talk with him. Hold your cup in your hands, and silently ask God for something you need his help with.**

Pray: **God, it is amazing that you know the needs of each of these children. Help them with the needs they are praying about right now.** Pause for a moment for the children to pray silently. **I am so grateful for the Bible that shows how much you care for us and for the example of answering the prayer of the servant as he searched for a wife for Isaac. Help us to remember to pray for your help always. In Jesus' name, amen.**

Jacob Deceives Esau and Isaac

Topic: Lying

Scripture: Genesis 25:19-24; 27:1-40

Simple Supplies: You'll need a Bible, a large candy bar, and candy treats for all.

Open your Bible to Genesis 25, and show the children the words. Say: **Today's Bible story is about twins—Jacob and Esau. Are any of you twins? Do you know any twins? When their dad, Isaac, was about to die, he wanted to give his sons his blessings. The oldest son always got the blessing that made him the head of the family. But the younger of the twins, Jacob, cheated the older, Esau. Jacob pretended to be his brother so his father would bless him instead of his brother. That wasn't fair!**

Let's play a game, and I'll show you what it might have felt like. Call up a volunteer, and whisper in his or her ear to come straight to you, no matter what you say during the game. When it starts, have the volunteer come straight to you.

OK! Let's play a quick game of Mother, May I. Whoever reaches me first will win this giant candy bar! Line up the kids opposite you, and say: **Take two giant steps forward.** The children will respond, "Mother, may I?" You may choose to say "yes" or "no." It doesn't matter, because the child you chose earlier will simply walk straight to you. When he or she reaches you, make a big deal out of giving the child the candy bar. Wait for other kids' responses. Ask:

- **How did it feel to have someone win by cheating?**
- **How do you think Esau felt when he discovered his brother got the special blessing by cheating?**

Say: **God wants us to tell the truth. Many bad things happen when we lie or when we cheat others. Because of Jacob's lie, his entire family split up. Jacob had to leave his family and go to live far away from his brother, mother, and father.**

Don't lie or cheat. Do what's right. When we follow God's teachings, we'll do what's right.

Play Mother, May I one more time. Say: **Say a prayer.** Have kids respond, "Mother, may I?" and say: **Yes!** Let any child who wishes to pray aloud do so.

Close by praying: **Thank you, God, for these children who want to follow your way and not cheat or lie. Strengthen them, help them follow your ways. In Jesus' name, amen.**

Distribute a piece of candy to each child.

 A leader was explaining that all Bibles begin with the book of Genesis. A puzzled little girl said, "My Bible doesn't begin with Genesis. It begins with Preface."

Joseph Tells His Dreams (1)

Topic: Families

Scripture: Genesis 37:1-11

Simple Supplies: You'll need a child-friendly Bible and a white board and marker or a chalkboard and chalk.

Open the child-friendly Bible to Genesis 37:1-11, and read about Joseph telling his dreams to his brothers. Say: **Joseph had a dream that one day his brothers and whole family would bow down to him! Joseph was telling his brothers that he would become more important than them. His brothers didn't like that. They hated him and didn't want anything to do with him. But that's not the way God wants families to treat each other. Families should work together and help each other. The brothers didn't understand that the dream was a way of God showing the plans he had for Joseph.**

Ask the kids to tell you what chores they do, what chores their brothers or sisters do, and things that their parents or guardians do. Make three columns on the white board or chalkboard—one column titled "My Chores," another column titled "My Brothers' and Sisters' Chores," and the last one labeled "My Parents' Chores." Chores could be "reading a bedtime story to my baby sister," "cleaning my room," "cleaning the bathroom," or "vacuuming the car."

Say: **A modern-day story of Joseph telling his dreams might go like this: "Hey, family. I had a dream that all of you had to do my chores as well as your chores!"** Make a big X through the "My Chores" column. Draw big arrows from the "My Chores" column to the other ones. Ask:

- **How would you feel if a brother or sister told you this?**
- **How do you think the brothers felt when Joseph told him his dreams?**

Say: **In a family, sometimes jealousy happens. Bad feelings happen. Families need to help each other and treat each other with love.**

Have the children join hands in a circle. Pray: **Dear God, thank you for showing us in the Bible about Joseph and his brothers. Help our families work together and find ways to show love to each other. Help us not be jealous of the plans you have for each person in our families. In Jesus' name, amen.**

Joseph Tells His Dreams (2)

Topic: Jealousy

Scripture: Genesis 37:1-11

Simple Supplies: You'll need a Bible.

Gather the children, and ask how many of them dream. Say: **I dream a lot. Sometimes I dream about things that are totally unbelievable, and sometimes I wake up in the morning and think, "What do you suppose that dream meant?"** Open your Bible to Genesis 37, and show the children the words. **The Bible tells** us about Joseph when he was a teenager. Joseph had some dreams. He also had lots of older brothers. Raise your hands if you have brothers. Pause. **Well, these brothers didn't like Joseph, and were sometimes very mean to him. Most of the time they fought because they were jealous of Joseph. Their father and Joseph had a very special relationship.**

One night Joseph had a dream. We're going to act out the dream right now. Who wants to be Joseph? Ask a volunteer to stand, then gather everyone in a circle around him or her. Have the kids do what you do. Raise your hands in the air, then bow down low to Joseph. Do this several times, then have everyone sit back down again. Ask:

- **What do you think Joseph's dream meant?**

Say: **Joseph dreamed that his brothers were all bowing down to him. He knew they didn't like him and were jealous of him, but the dream showed them making him special. When Joseph told his brothers the dream, they were even more jealous and upset with Joseph!** Ask:

- **When have you been jealous?**
- **When has someone been jealous of you?**

Say: **Sometimes we're jealous of brothers or sisters or friends who get more attention or seem more talented than we are. Sometimes people are jealous of us for the same reasons. God doesn't want us to be jealous. God wants us to show love to others.**

A lot of sad things happened to Joseph because of the jealousy in this story, but God eventually brought good out of a bad thing. Joseph's brothers did bow down to him later, and he was able to save them from starving. When we feel jealousy toward someone, we need to stop and give our feelings to God. God wants us to love others, not be jealous.

Have the children form a circle and bow down again, but this time to God. Pray: **God, we know you understand that sometimes we can feel jealous. We want to love others like you do. Help us when we have jealous feelings. Thank you for how you use all things to bring glory to your name. In Jesus' name, amen.**

Joseph Is Sold Into Slavery (1)

Topic: God's Plans

Scripture: Genesis 37:12-36

Simple Supplies: You'll need a Bible, chairs, upbeat music, and a box.

Open your Bible to Genesis 37, and show the children the words. Say: **Today's story is about Joseph and his family. Joseph's dad gave him a colorful coat. Joseph had lots of older brothers. Did the brothers get cool coats too? No way! The brothers were jealous of Joseph. They finally couldn't take it anymore.**

One day, the brothers threw Joseph in a pit. Then they sold Joseph to be a slave and told their dad that Joseph had died. How could God let that happen? But hold on a minute! God had everything planned for Joseph, his family, and an entire country! It didn't seem so happy, because no one could see God's plans. Let's play a game and see what Joseph must have felt like.

Set out enough chairs so there are enough for all the children, but not for you. Tell the children that when the music stops, they all have to sit on a chair. Say: **Whoever doesn't get a chair is out.** Play the music, then stop it. Look frantically for a chair, and be the one who is left without a chair. Tell the kids to "throw" you in the "pit," which is the box. Stand in the box and say: **I'll just stay here in this pit and ask you a couple of questions.** Ask:

- **How do you think I felt when I was put in this box?**
- **How do you think Joseph felt when his brothers got mad and put him in a pit?**

Say: **At first Joseph must have been afraid. His brothers sold him to be a slave in a different country, but God had plans for Joseph so everything he did in that country turned out well. In fact, after many years, he was made a ruler in that new country. Joseph helped save that country, and even his brothers, from starving when there was no food. God's plan was in place even when it looked like God was letting bad things happen.**

Let's say a prayer, telling God we trust his plans to make good things happen. Step out of the box and say: **Dear God, help me to trust you to have a plan for good even when things look bad.** One by one, each child should go into the pit, then step out and say, "Dear God, help me to trust you to have a good plan."

Joseph Is Sold Into Slavery (2)

Topic: Good Will Come

Scripture: Genesis 37:12-36

Simple Supplies: You'll need a Bible and a brightly colored coat.

Say: **Let's talk about how God can make good things come out of bad. Let's think about some bad things that turned out good. Can anyone think of one?** Pause, then share a personal story similar to one of these examples. **I can! When I was little, I loved it when we had a big, huge snowstorm. It meant that no one could go anyplace—my parents couldn't go to work, we had to shovel snow for hours, and we couldn't even go to school. Now that snow might have seemed bad to some people, but to me it seemed great! I got a vacation day from school.**

Here's another one. I know a man who had a bad disease. He almost died, but God allowed him to live. The man was so thankful to God that he became a famous speaker. Now he goes all over the country telling about this illness and God's love for him and others. God used a bad thing to let more people know that God loves them. Ask:

- **How can we help others know that God brings good from bad things?**

Open your Bible to Genesis 37:12-36, and show the children the words. Say: **The Bible tells us about Joseph. You may have heard** about him before. He had lots of brothers who were jealous of him. His brothers thought their dad loved Joseph more than he loved them. One day their father gave Joseph a beautiful coat of many colors. Kind of like this one! Ask a volunteer to put on the coat and stand in front of the others. **Other people who saw Joseph might have said, "Look at Joseph. He looks so handsome." That could have made his brothers even more jealous.** Ask:

- **When have you been jealous?**
- **When has someone been jealous of you?**

Say: **You know what the brothers did? They made a plan to get rid of Joseph. When their father wasn't looking, they took Joseph's coat.** Take the coat from the volunteer. **Then they put Joseph in a well, which is a deep hole, until they could decide what to do with him.** Ask "Joseph" to sit on the floor. Then have everyone form a tight circle around him and raise their arms high, like a high wall of a well. Ask:

- **How do you feel down there Joseph?** Pause for the child to answer.

Say: **The brothers took Joseph out of the well and sold him to some travelers going to Egypt.** Have all the children sit down. **You know what? God makes good things come from bad. God was watching out for Joseph. Joseph worked for Pharaoh who was like a king. Eventually Joseph helped many, many people live through a famine, which is a time when there is no rain and very little food. There is a lot more in the Bible that tells how much good Joseph did because he was in Egypt in his position!**

Ask everyone to gather around so they each can hold onto the coat. Pray: **Dear God, thanks for making good come from a bad thing in Joseph's life. Help us trust you to make good come from bad things. We trust you with our whole lives. In Jesus' name, amen.**

LEADER

Combine this message with "Joseph Tells His Dreams." It's especially effective for the kids to experience Joseph standing tall in the center of brothers who are bowing to him, then Joseph sitting in a well with a tall wall of children around him. God does make good things happen out of bad!

God Keeps Baby Moses Safe

Topic: God's Care

Scripture: Exodus 1—2:10

Simple Supplies: You'll need a Bible, a clear drinking glass or jar, paper napkins (enough for each child plus one), and a tub of water.

Stuff a napkin inside the glass, show it to the kids, and ask:

- **If I put this glass upside down into the water, what do you think will happen to the napkin?**

Say: **Those are some good thoughts. In a few minutes we'll try it and see what happens. This experiment reminds me of when Moses was a baby.** Open your Bible to Exodus 1, and show the children the words.

Pharaoh was the leader of the land. He wanted to kill all the Hebrew baby boys because there were so many Hebrews that he was afraid they'd grow up to become his enemies and fight against him. Moses' mother protected him. She made a waterproof basket and put Moses inside. Then she hid the basket in the tall grasses of the river.

Pharaoh's own daughter saw the basket and had it brought to shore. Imagine her surprise when she discovered a baby inside! She kept the baby and named him Moses. Then she hired Moses' mother (not knowing she was his mother) to take care of him until he was ready to live with her in the palace.

Let's try our experiment now and see what happens to the napkin in the glass. Dip the glass upside down and straight into the water, then pull it up and have kids examine the napkin. Ask:

- **What happened to the napkin?**
- **Why did it stay dry?**

Say: **There is an invisible helper that protected the napkin and kept it dry. That helper is air! Air was trapped inside the glass and had nowhere to go, so it made a barrier between the water and the napkin. Moses' family must have been scared with such** a cruel Pharaoh ruling their land, but God cared for them. Just like air is invisible to us, God was invisible to Moses and his family, and like the air protected the napkin, God was there all along, protecting them. Ask:

- **When are you afraid?**
- **How can you remember that God is always with you caring for you?**

Say: **Just like with Moses, God doesn't always take us out of a problem situation, but he always makes a way to be with us and take care of us. God can take care of us in amazing ways, even when it seems impossible. I have a napkin here for each of you as a way of remembering that even when we don't know it, God is with us taking care of us.**

Give each child a napkin as you pray: **Dear God, thank you for the way you took care of Moses. Thank you that you are with us taking care of us, too. Help us remember your care each day. In Jesus' name, amen.**

Moses Meets God at the Burning Bush

Topic: Meeting God

Scripture: Exodus 2:11–3:20

Simple Supplies: You'll need a Bible, metal garbage can or large roasting pan, paper, and a lighter or match.

Gather the children, then ask:

- **When you're watching TV or playing a game and your parents want you for something, what do they do to get your attention?**

LEADER TIP

This message involves using flame. Safety first! Be sure the container you use is clean and fireproof. Also, present this message where smoke and heat won't set off a smoke detector or sprinkler system.

Say: **What a lot of ways to get your attention! Well, the Bible tells us that one time God wanted to get Moses' attention. And, as God often does, he did it in an amazing way.**

Start a piece of paper on fire, and hold it over the garbage can while it burns, then drop it in the can. Say: **Do I have your attention? I'm sure you didn't expect me to start a fire here today! Moses didn't expect God to do what he did either. God spoke to Moses from a bush that was on fire but didn't burn up. That got Moses' attention all right.** Let the kids look at the paper in the garbage can and notice what condition it's in. **When something's on fire, it burns up. Moses saw the fire and realized it wasn't burning up the bush. Then he heard God talking to him, and he was amazed and in awe. He fell to his knees, worshipped, and talked with God.**

God needed to get Moses' attention because he had a special job for him to do. God wanted Moses to lead his people out of Egypt and into the Promised Land! Ask:

- **What would you have done if you saw the burning bush?**
- **What did God want Moses to do?**
- **How does God get our attention?**
- **What does God want us to do?**

Say: **I think I'd have been like Moses and fallen on my knees if I'd seen the burning bush! God had a big job for Moses and got his attention in a big way. God gets our attention through prayer, worship, church, and other Christians. And one thing God wants all of his followers to do is to use our gifts and tell others how much he loves them. We all have important jobs to do!**

Have the children hold their arms up and wiggle their fingers like a bush on fire as you pray.

Pray: **Lord, help us to learn about you and what you want us to do. Help us to obey, just as Moses did. In Jesus' name, amen.**

Moses Pleads With Pharaoh

Topic: God's Plans

Scripture: Exodus 7:14–12:30

Simple Supplies: You'll need a Bible, overhead projector, transparency from page 49, and overhead marker, or poster board and marker. Photocopy the handout (p. 49) onto a transparency or draw it on a piece of poster board.

Say: **We all have wanted some things and not gotten them. Sometimes we want things like a video game or a new toy, something that's just for fun. But sometimes we want really important things like for a friend who's sick to get better or for our parents to get back together.**

Open your Bible to Exodus 7, and show kids the words. Say: **Moses was in a situation like that. God gave Moses a big job. God wanted to free his people from being slaves to the cruel Pharaoh. Moses very much wanted this to happen too. But that meant Moses would be leading over a million people out of Egypt and away from Pharaoh. It meant leading them through a desert and into the land God promised to give his people.**

How could Moses do it? Well, Moses knew a secret that I'm going to show you. See if you can figure out what the secret is.

Turn on the overhead projector showing the transparency you prepared beforehand. Choose a volunteer to point to squares on the transparency as you give instructions. Say: [Name of child], **touch any gray square. Now move either left or right and touch the nearest clear square.** Pause. **Now move up or down, your choice, and touch the nearest gray square.** Pause. **Now move diagonally to the nearest clear square.** Pause. **Now move left or right to the nearest gray square.** Pause. **Good job! We ended up at "God." Let's have someone else try it.** Choose another volunteer and repeat the game. **Now let's give the rest of you a turn. Using your eyes, look at the squares as I give you the instructions again.** Repeat the instructions, then ask kids where they always end up in the game.

No matter what box you start with, you end up at "God"! That's the secret—whenever you're facing a tough situation like Moses was, do what he did—trust and obey God. God is always in control, no matter how impossible things seem. That's because he's bigger and stronger than anyone or anything. He always knows the plan, just like I knew the plan for the way to make sure you always ended up at "God" in the game we played. Ask:

- What's a problem you have right now?
- How can you trust that God is in control and has a plan?

Say: **No matter what problems we face, we need to pray and trust that God is in control.** Close by having kids think of problems that they want to give to God. Ask a volunteer to play the game again. When the volunteer lands on "God," lead all the children in praying: **We give our problems to you. We trust you are in control and have a plan for us. In Jesus' name, amen.**

Moses Crosses the Red Sea

Topic: Miracles

Scripture: Exodus 13:17–14:31

Simple Supplies: You'll need a Bible, a cookie sheet with edges, aluminum foil, food coloring, a glass of water, a bowl of rubbing alcohol, and a spoon. Line the pan with aluminum foil and add food coloring to the glass of water. Practice the experiment ahead of time so you know what to expect.

Say: **I have an experiment to try with you today that makes us move water without touching it. Let's see how it works.** Have kids gather around the pan. Pour a thin layer of the colored water onto the foil. **I've put some colored water in this pan. Now I'm going to add a little of this rubbing alcohol to the water. Watch what happens.** Drop a small amount of rubbing alcohol from the spoon into

Moses Pleads With Pharaoh

A 4×3 grid with alternating shaded and white cells. The cell in the second row, fourth column contains the word "God".

Permission to photocopy this page from *The Humongous Book of Children's Messages* granted for local church use. Copyright © Group Publishing, Inc., P.O. Box 481, Loveland, CO 80539.
www.grouppublishing.com

the center of the water. **What did the water do? Did you see it move out of the way?** Add a few more drops of alcohol so kids can watch it again. **The molecules in the water and the rubbing alcohol react to each other, pushing away from each other. This makes it look like the water is moving out of the way. It's a chemical reaction that looks pretty cool. But it doesn't even come close to comparing to how God moved water for the Israelites.**

Open your Bible to Exodus 13, and show the children the words. Say: **God's people had escaped from Pharaoh, who (along with the Pharaohs before him) had kept the people in slavery for over four hundred years. At first Pharaoh said they could leave, but then he changed his mind and chased after them with his army. Pharaoh was a powerful and mean man and would stop at nothing to get his way. He was going to teach those Israelites a lesson!**

Just then, Moses and the people came to the Red Sea. There was no way across. They couldn't go back because Pharaoh was coming to kill them. Moses told them to be brave and trust God. And then God did an incredible thing. He parted the deep waters of the Red Sea, and the people walked across on dry land! That was not some little chemical reaction. That was a miracle! Ask:

- **What are other miracles you know from the Bible?**
- **How do you think God does these miracles?**

Say: **God does amazing things! That's because he's creator of all things! Aren't you glad you serve a God who's so strong and powerful? And the best part is, we can ask God for help! So when you feel like you've got nowhere to go, call out to God and trust him to help. He can do amazing things for you, just as he did for Moses and his people.**

Pray: **Thank you God, for the wonderful miracles you have shown us in the Bible. Help us to see the miracles around us that you do each day.** Drip one more drop of alcohol into the pan, and ask kids to say with you: **In Jesus' name, amen.**

God Gives Moses the Ten Commandments

Topic: Rules

Scripture: Exodus 20:1-17; Matthew 22:36-40

Simple Supplies: You'll need a Bible, a child car seat, and a bike helmet.

Say: **Rules, rules, rules—they're everywhere! Don't run in church, be quiet when Dad is taking a nap, chew with your mouth closed, no gum in school, and wash your hands before you eat.** Hold up the child car seat, and then the bike helmet. For each one, ask these questions:

- **What rule does this item remind you of?**
- **Why do we have that rule?**

Say: **A small child needs to be strapped into a car seat so the child will be safe in case of an accident. An older kid needs to wear a bike helmet to keep the kid's head safe in case of an accident. Rules show us how to live, and they keep us safe. God knew that long ago when he gave Moses the Ten Commandments.**

Open your Bible to Exodus 20, and show it to the children. Say: **Here are the Ten Commandments, written down for everyone to read. If we're honest, all of us have trouble keeping rules sometimes. Since we're human and God made us, he knew we'd have a hard time! That's why God sent Jesus.**

Turn in your Bible to Matthew 22:36-40, then read the passage out loud to the kids. **Jesus picked out the greatest of the commandments. He said we are to love God above all else and our neighbor as ourselves.** Ask:

- **What's it mean to love God above all else?**
- **What's it mean to love our neighbor as ourselves?**

Say: **If we love God above all else, we make him number one in our lives. We focus on him, we pray to him, we trust him** completely. When we love our neighbors as ourselves, we treat them kindly and we care for them.

Ask kids to each hold up a pointer finger as "number one." Pray: **Dear God, please help us keep you number one in our lives.** Then ask kids to hug a neighbor. **Please help us love our neighbors as ourselves. In Jesus' name, amen.**

Moses Sends Spies Into the Promised Land

Topic: Trusting God

Scripture: Numbers 13:1–14:23

Simple Supplies: You'll need a Bible, purple or green balloons, green yarn, a yardstick, and binoculars. Inflate the balloons, and string them together with the yarn. Then loop them over the middle of the yardstick to look like a giant cluster of grapes.

Open your Bible to Numbers 13, then show the children the words.

Say: **After the Israelites left Egypt, God made them a promise that seemed too good to be true. He said he'd give them a special place to live, a land flowing with milk and honey. That meant it was a good land for food and everything they'd need to raise their families.**

God told Moses to send someone to check out the new land. So Moses sent Caleb and Joshua and ten other men to be spies and see what the land was like.

Look through the binoculars at the kids, then at the balloon grapes. Say: **They saw some amazing things.**

Have two kids hold the yardstick of "grapes" at each end. Say: **When the men came back, they brought some samples of the fruit they found in the land.** Ask the kids to hold up the cluster of grapes.

In that land, the fruit was so huge that one cluster of grapes had to be carried on a pole between two people! They couldn't believe all the food that was there.

Though it was a good land, just as God said, there were some problems. Big problems, in fact. The land was filled with giant people! The Bible says the spies felt like grasshoppers compared to them. This terrified the rest of the Israelites, who felt the giants were too strong for them. They didn't trust God to help them.

The Israelites cried and complained, but Caleb and Joshua weren't afraid. They reminded the people that God always keeps his promises. If God said they could take the land, then they could! God would help them and they wouldn't fail. They trusted God would do what he said.

Because of their faith, Joshua and Caleb were allowed to enter the land. The others who had complained weren't allowed to go into the land. Ask:

- How did Joshua and Caleb show they trusted God?
- How can we trust God always?

Say: **Joshua and Caleb trusted God when he said he'd give them the land, no matter what problems—like giants—they had to face. When we face problems, we can pray to God and trust that he'll see us through.**

Look through the binoculars during the prayer. Look at each child, and then look at the adults in the congregation. Pray: **Dear God thank you for these children and the adults who love and care for them. Help us to trust you when we face problems. You are awesome and we are grateful that we can trust your love for us. In Jesus' name, amen.**

Balaam's Donkey Talks

Topic: God Knows Our Hearts

Scripture: Numbers 22

Simple Supplies: You'll need a Bible and a balloon.

Blow up the balloon in front of the kids. Hold the end tightly so the air doesn't leak out. Say: **I have a message for you today.** Stretch the opening of the balloon, letting the air out so that the balloon squawks loudly. **Did anyone understand the message? Of course not; I was being silly! But one time God spoke to a man in a stranger way than that.**

Open your Bible to Numbers 22, and show the kids the words. Say: **God had a donkey talk to a man one time! I'm not kidding you; it's in the Bible. The man's name was Balaam and he wasn't listening to God, so God chose to use his donkey to speak to him. How strange is that? But let me back up a bit.**

You see, there was a king in a certain country who considered Balaam a prophet, someone who speaks with God. He wanted Balaam to pray and curse the Israelites so that they wouldn't be able to fight successfully against his people. The king promised Balaam lots of gold and silver.

Balaam said he wouldn't curse the Israelites because they were God's people. But he got on his donkey and rode to meet the king anyway. That made God angry. He knew what was in Balaam's heart—that he cared more about money than about doing what pleased God.

On the road to the king's palace, God sent an angel to stop Balaam. Balaam couldn't see the angel, but his donkey could! The donkey stopped and refused to move. Balaam began to beat the donkey! Then the Lord opened the donkey's mouth and she spoke!

Release more air from the balloon and make it squawk lightly while you say the donkey's words.

Say: **She said, "Don't hurt me. Am I not your faithful donkey that you've always ridden? Have I ever done this to you before?" Then Balaam saw the angel. If the donkey hadn't stopped him, the angel would've killed him. Not only did the donkey speak, she saved Balaam's life. Balaam was sorry, and after that he tried to do what God told him.** Ask:

- What surprised you about this story?
- How does God know what's in our hearts?

Say: **God knew what was in Balaam's heart. He knows what's in our hearts. So you don't have to pretend to be something you're not with God. God loves you just the way you are. Let's make sure we do only what God tells us to do—just like Balaam's donkey did!**

Blow the balloon up again, and after the prayer as the children are leaving, let each one let a little air out of the balloon. Encourage them to tell God thank you for loving them just the way they are. Pray:

Dear God, thank you for showing us how you made the donkey talk to teach Balaam. I'm so glad you know my heart and that you love me just as I am. Help me tell others that they can know you and your love for them. In Jesus' name, amen.

Jericho's Walls Come Down

Topic: Obey God

Scripture: Joshua 6:1-27

Simple Supplies: You'll need a Bible, two balloons, a straight pin, and transparent tape. Inflate the balloons three-fourths full, and tie them off.

Hold up one of the balloons and the pin, then ask:

- **Who thinks I can push this pin into the balloon without popping it?**
- **Would any of you like to try?**

Have a volunteer try it. Say: **It's impossible, isn't it? Many things in our lives seem impossible.**

Open your Bible to Joshua 6:1-27, and show the children the words.

Say: **Joshua felt that he had something impossible to do too. God told him to conquer the city of Jericho. Jericho was built high up on a mound of earth. Its walls were so high and thick that people built their homes inside of them. It didn't seem possible for Joshua and his small army to take such a strong city. But Joshua trusted God and obeyed him, even when God told him to do a hard thing.**

God told Joshua to march around the city with his full army once a day for six days, and the priests were to blow trumpets.

Ask the kids to stand and turn in a circle six times.

Say: **On the seventh day, they were to march around the city seven times, with the priests blowing the trumpets. When the trumpets sounded a long blast, all the people were to give a loud shout.**

Have kids march in place, make a trumpet sound, and then shout.

Say: **Joshua and the people obeyed, and the walls of the city totally collapsed! The people were able to go up the mound and straight into the city. God's instructions worked!**

That brings me back to the balloon. I read in a book how to put a pin in the balloon without making it pop. So it might be possible after all, if we follow the instructions. Let's try.

Make an X shape on the balloon with two pieces of tape. Hold the balloon firmly, and carefully insert the pin through the center of the tape. Hold up the balloon and show kids the pin.

Say: **It worked! I followed the instructions and had success. That's how it was for Joshua at Jericho. He obeyed God's instructions, and everything turned out as he said it would. You know, God can do anything.** Ask:

- **Why do you think Joshua obeyed God?**
- **How can we obey God?**

Say: **Joshua obeyed, so he and the small army of the Israelites conquered the city of Jericho. We can obey God by listening to** his words from the Bible, by obeying our parents or guardians, and by telling everyone about Jesus. God does mighty things when we obey him.

Have the children pass the balloon around so each child gets a chance to see the pin in the balloon while you pray: **Dear God, I am so glad that you give us instructions on how to live life. Thank you for the example of Joshua and how he obeyed your instructions. Help me learn and obey what you want me to do. In Jesus' name, amen.**

God Gives Gideon Victory

Topic: God Helps

Scripture: Judges 6:1-16; 7:1-24

Simple Supplies: You'll need a Bible, a table, three large canned food items, and lots of cotton balls.

Open your Bible to Judges 6, and show the children the words. Say: **God told Gideon to save God's people, the Israelites, from their enemies. But Gideon didn't think he could do it. The enemies were big, and he was small. They were strong, and he was weak.** Set the three big cans of food in a row. **These cans represent the big enemies.** Place a cotton ball next to the cans. **Imagine that this cotton ball is Gideon.** Ask:

• **Who's bigger, stronger, and tougher?** Have a child cover the cotton ball with one of the cans, smashing it.

Say: **That's how Gideon felt in comparison to the enemies. But God sent an angel to tell Gideon that God would be with him and that he could do it. God assured Gideon several times that it was going to be OK.**

Have another child dump a big pile of cotton balls out on the table. Say: **Gideon's army was big—thirty-two thousand men! But God said, no, that's too many—make it three hundred.** Have a couple of children help you clear away all but three of the cotton balls and stand them facing the large cans. **It seemed impossible. And that's just how God wanted it. God wanted everyone to know that he was the reason the Israelites would defeat their enemies. Gideon obeyed God. Gideon and his men beat their enemies. When God promises you something, you can expect him to do it.** Ask:

- **What seemed impossible in the story?**
- **What seems impossible in your life?**

Say: **Sometimes we might be afraid to face something, like Gideon was afraid at first to face the enemies. God helped Gideon, and God helps us.**

Give each child a cotton ball. Say: **Close your eyes and silently tell God about a fear or problem that you are facing.** Pause, then pray: **Dear God, thank you for helping Gideon, and thank you for helping us. We praise you and thank you, in Jesus' name, amen.**

God Gives Samson a Special Gift

Topic: Gifts

Scripture: Judges 15:9-16; 16:4-30

Simple Supplies: You'll need a Bible and several current superhero action figures.

Gather the children, and one at a time show them the action figures you've brought with you. With each action figure, ask:

- **Who is this superhero?**
- **What makes the superhero strong?**
- **What is this superhero's weakness?**

Open your Bible to Judges 15, and show the children the words. Say: **The Bible tells about a real superhero named Samson. Samson was a leader of God's people. God gave Samson the gift of strength. And, wow, was Samson strong! Samson was so strong that he picked up a bone of a donkey and struck down one thousand men.** Compare that number to the number of people who are in your room. **Samson fell in love with Delilah. She wanted to trick Samson and find out why he was so strong. Some people who wanted to capture and hurt Samson said they'd pay Delilah a lot of money if she'd trick him. Samson told Delilah that God had given him the gift of strength. He told her that if someone cut his long hair short, he would lose his strength. Delilah led Samson's enemies to cut his hair.** Ask kids to touch their hair. **His enemies captured Samson, and then they blinded him.** Ask kids to close their eyes. **Then they took him to prison. Samson was in prison for a while and had to work very hard. His hair grew back, and his heart was sorry! Samson's enemies wanted him to entertain them. So his enemies brought Samson to where everyone was gathered. They stood him between two pillars that held up the building. Samson asked God to give him the gift of strength one more time and God did. Samson pushed on the pillars that were holding up the area where all his enemies were.** Have kids push their arms out as if pushing over two pillars. **The wall toppled on top of all of Samson's enemies. Samson used his gift of strength to conquer his enemies.** Ask:

- **How did Samson use his gift of strength for God?**
- **What gifts does God give you?**

Say: **God gave Samson the gift of strength. He used it to beat his enemies. God gives us many gifts. We can use our gifts to tell people about God who loves us so.**

Have the children make strong arm muscles while you pray: **Dear God, thanks for all the wonderful gifts you give us. Help us learn how to use those gifts the way you want us to. We love you and want to help others know you. In Jesus' name, amen.**

Ruth Trusts God

Topic: Welcoming Everyone

Scripture: Ruth 2–4

Simple Supplies: You'll need a Bible, a marker, and three sheets of poster board. Write each of these "words" on separate sheets: "Sagoogled," "Varumpt," "Badanglang."

Say: **Welcome everyone! Let's pretend for a moment that you've traveled a long way around the world and you've come to a new country. Pretend that you're hungry and you're trying to find some place to eat. You walk up to a person, say "Where's a place to eat?" and the person says to you, "Sagoogled."** Hold up the poster board with the made-up word on it. Have all the children repeat the word after you, and ask a child to stand and hold the word. Look puzzled. **Huh? What's that supposed to mean?**

Well, then you walk to someone else, and this person tells you, "Varumpt." Have the children repeat the word after you, and ask a child to stand and hold up that poster board. **Huh? How frustrating!**

So you go to someone else, and that person says, "Badang-lang." Again have the children repeat the word, and ask a child to stand and hold up that poster board. **Huh? How in the world would you get something to eat if you couldn't understand the words people were saying?** Ask:

- **How would you feel if you were in a new country and couldn't understand people?**
- **How would you get along?**

Ask children holding the poster boards to put them aside and sit back down. Open your Bible to Ruth, and show kids the words. Say: **I think I might be scared if I couldn't understand people, but I'd trust that God is with me, and I'd try to find someone to help me! Well, the Bible tells about a person who went to a new country and trusted God to take care of her. Ruth's husband had died and so had her father-in-law. She had no one to live** with except her husband's mother, her mother-in-law, Naomi. But Naomi felt she should return to the country her husband was from. So Ruth went with Naomi to Bethlehem.

Ruth and Naomi were hungry but didn't have any money to buy food. A man named Boaz realized that Ruth and Naomi were new to the place. Boaz welcomed them, helped them get food, and protected them. Ask:

- **Why might people need to move to a new area?**
- **How can we welcome people who are new to our area?**

Say: **People often move to new places. Let's watch for new kids in our neighborhoods, schools, and church, and let's welcome them like Boaz welcomed Ruth and Naomi. Invite them to play, invite them to worship, and invite them to your homes to eat. God wants us to welcome all, because when we welcome others, we show God's love to them.**

Have the children each find a partner and link elbows with the partner as you close with prayer: **Dear God, thank you for showing us the example of Boaz being kind to Ruth and Naomi when they needed help in a new place. Help us to notice the new people who come to our neighborhoods, schools, and church. Help us be kind and loving to them. In Jesus' name, amen.**

Samuel Listens to God

Topic: God's Voice

Scripture: 1 Samuel 3:1-21

Simple Supplies: You'll need a Bible, an old telephone, duct tape, two clean soup cans, and a long length of string. Make a play telephone by poking a hole in the bottom of each can, threading the string through the holes, and tying each end of the string in a knot. Cover the cans' edges with duct tape to avoid cuts.

Go to a local thrift store
or Salvation Army.
Find a variety of old
telephones—the older
the better. Remember
the circular dials and
the cords?

Ask the children what they use when they need to contact someone. Say: **We might call people on telephones, cell phones, and pagers, or send them an e-mail.** Mention other things kids said. **I've brought with me some ways that people used to talk to each other.** Show them your old telephone. **Have any of you ever seen such an old telephone?**

Let me show you another way to communicate. Show the children your play phone of two tin cans connected by string. **I need a volunteer to take one end of our play phone and stand as far away from me as possible, with the string tight.** Wait for the child to get in position. **Place the can to your ear, and repeat what I'm about to say into this end of the phone.** As softly as possible, say into the can: **God loves you.** Do this several times, and each time speak a little louder until your message is finally heard. Then ask the child to return to the group.

Sometimes we have to repeat what we say so others can hear and understand. Open your Bible to 1 Samuel 3:1-21, and say: **When**

Samuel was a boy, he was sleeping in the Tabernacle where he worked for God. At night, he heard a voice calling his name. He thought it was the Temple priest calling him. But it wasn't. No, it was God's voice! Finally, after the Temple priest explained what to do, Samuel said, "Speak, for your servant is listening." And then God talked with Samuel and told him many important things. Ask:

- **How does God speak to us?**
- **What are things God tells us to do?**

Say: **God spoke to Samuel at night and called his name. God speaks to us through worship, Christian friends, prayer, songs, and the Bible. Let's listen to God and tell others about him too.**

Let kids use the play phone to whisper "God loves you" to each other. Close in prayer by speaking into the play phone. Pray: **Hello, God. I am so glad that you hear my prayers no matter how I try to talk to you. I want to hear what you want to tell me. Help** me to listen to you in the Bible, when I pray, and when other Christians talk to me. Remind me to tell others they can know you and hear from you too. In Jesus' name, amen.

David Becomes King

Topic: God Knows Our Hearts

Scripture: 1 Samuel 16:1-13

Simple Supplies: You'll need a Bible.

Open your Bible to 1 Samuel 16:1-13, and show the children the words. Say: **Today's Bible story is about God choosing a person to be king! A king is a ruler or the number-one leader of a country. Wow! A king!** Ask:

- **If you were choosing someone to lead our country, what kinds of things would you look for?**

Say: **Let's pretend we're looking for a leader for our country. We'd want the leader to be** [use characteristics the children mentioned when you asked the question, such as smart, strong, and wise]. With each word you use to describe the person, ask the kids to stand taller and taller and taller. After everyone is standing tall, say: **Yes! That's what we'd want for a leader of our country!**

Let the kids sit down again. Say: **In our Bible story, God sent Samuel to find a new king or a leader for God's people. God sent Samuel to Jesse, who was the father of many wonderful sons. When he looked at the sons, it seemed like any one was fit to be a king.** Ask the kids to stand tall. **Samuel looked at all these wonderful sons, but knew that the one God wanted to be king wasn't one of them. So as he looked at each son, he said, "No, this isn't the one."** Have the children get in a line, and look at each one and say, **No, this isn't the one.** Have the children sit down one at a time after you say that to each one.

Samuel asked if Jesse had any other sons. Jesse said that there was only the youngest son who wasn't there because he was taking care of his family's sheep. Samuel asked to see this youngest son. Ask the kids to crouch down as small as they can get and say, "I'm little David."

When Samuel saw the youngest son David, he said, "Yes! This is our new king!" Ask:

- **What surprised you about our Bible story?**
- **Would you have thought God would pick young David to be king? Why or why not?**

Say: **David was a boy, maybe even your age. But God told Samuel that David was who he wanted to lead his people. David? The youngest son? The one who was taking care of the sheep? God didn't look at how old David was. God didn't look at how small David was. God didn't look at the job David was doing. God knows what we are like on the inside. God knew David had a good heart and that David loved him. So God chose David to be king.**

Close by having the kids stand tall again. Pray: **Dear God, we might be tempted to see how people look on the outside—tall, strong, and talented.** Have kids crouch. **You look at our hearts and how much we love you. Thank you! It's the inside that counts!** Have kids stand again. **Help us love you with our whole hearts, like David did. In Jesus' name, amen.**

David Defeats Goliath

Topic: Facing Fears

Scripture: 1 Samuel 17:1-51

Simple Supplies: Gather enough cardboard boxes to stack at least nine feet tall. You also will need a Bible, packing tape, and a step ladder (optional). Ask another adult to help you when it's time to stack the boxes.

Say: **Look at all these boxes! Let's organize them by stacking them on top of each other.** Have the children take turns bringing you the boxes. Allow them to put one on top of another until they can no longer reach the top. Let the kids attach tape to lightly connect the boxes. Have the adult help you and the children stack the boxes until the tower is approximately nine feet tall. **This is huge! Let's take turns standing next to the boxes. Wow! This is much taller than you and me.** As the kids are taking turns standing next to the tall stack of boxes, open your Bible to 1 Samuel 17. Wait until kids are seated before you continue.

The Bible tells about a man who was an enemy of God's people, the Israelites. His name was Goliath, and he was over nine feet tall, as tall as this stack of boxes! Exaggerate looking all the way up to the top of the stack of boxes. **Whoa! That's tall! Goliath and his bunch of fighters were making fun of God's people, and the Israelites were really afraid. No one in the Israelite army would fight Goliath.** Ask:

- **Why do you think the Israelites were afraid?**
- **When have you been really afraid?**

Say: **The Israelites were afraid because Goliath was tall and mean. We might be afraid when people pick on us or when we have to move to a new neighborhood. Finally, a young boy named David said he'd fight the giant. He knew how to use a sling, which was a piece of leather that would hold a stone. David put a stone in the sling. He twirled it around his head and flung the stone toward Goliath.** Have the kids pretend they're twirling a sling above their heads. **The Bible says the stone hit Goliath's forehead and he fell facedown dead.** Have the children help you take apart the stack of boxes so they are scattered on the floor again. **God helped young David beat the big giant Goliath!** Ask:

• **How can God help you face your fears?**

Say: **When you're facing something hard like the death of a favorite pet or** [add ideas the children have shared]**, remember to pray to God. Trust him to help you, just as he helped David beat Goliath.**

Let each child take a piece of the tape from the boxes. Say: **This tape is like the way God sticks to us when we're dealing with some fear or hard time.** Stick a piece of tape on your arm. **God wants us to talk to him about our fears so he can help us. Keep this piece of tape to remind you that God cares about what is going on in your life and wants to help you with whatever hard situation you might face. Stick the tape to yourself as we pray.** Pray: **Dear God, thank you that you stick close to me. Thank you that you want to help me with the "giants" in my life. Help me remember to turn to you in hard situations, just as David did when he faced Goliath. In Jesus' name, amen.**

David and Jonathan Are Friends

Topic: Friendship

Scripture: 1 Samuel 18:1-4; 19:1-7; 20:1-42

Simple Supplies: You'll need red poster board, 8½ x 11 sheets of paper, and a Bible. Cut the poster board into a large heart, and cut hearts from the paper (one heart per sheet of paper per child).

Say: **How many remember the Bible story of David and Goliath? The Bible says that young David beat the mean giant Goliath. The man who ruled over Israel at that time was King Saul. Now the king had a son named Jonathan, who became best friends with David.**

I have a big red heart. Hold up the poster board heart. **Hearts are a symbol of love.** Ask:

• **In what ways do best friends show they love each other?**

Allow time for children to respond. Answers could be "They help each other," "They listen to each other," "They play together," or "They pray for each other." When a child answers, hand the child a paper heart. Say: **Those are all great ways to show friends you love them. I love all of you, so I'll give each of you a paper heart.** Hand out the rest of the paper hearts.

Another way friends show they love each other is by giving each other presents. I love presents! Open the Bible to 1 Samuel 18, and point to it. **The Bible says that Jonathan gave his robe and sword to David. Think about it. Jonathan (who was a king's son) gave David (who was a servant at that time) good presents! What a great way for friends to show they love each other!** Have the children each make heartbeat sounds by using one hand to hold the paper heart on his or her chest then patting it with the other hand. Pat your poster board heart, too!

Another way Jonathan showed how much he loved David was by protecting him from his father, King Saul. King Saul wanted to hurt David because he was jealous of David. David was loved by the people of Israel more than Saul was. Jonathan protected his friend David. Wow! What a great way for friends to show they love each other! Make heartbeat sounds.

Let's show our friends here that we love them, too! Ask the children to hug someone close to them. Afterward, make heartbeat sounds. Ask them to hug someone else, then make heartbeat sounds. Finally, ask them to help someone sitting close by them to stand up. Then make heartbeat sounds.

Ask the children to hold their paper hearts close to their chests as you pray: **Dear God, thank you for our friends. Help us to show love to our friends like Jonathan showed to David. In Jesus' name, amen.**

Tell the children to keep their paper hearts in their Bibles or stick them to their refrigerator doors as a reminder that friends love each other.

Say: **Each time you see your paper heart this week, pray for a friend. Ask God to help you love your friends and treat them the way Jonathan treated David.**

Solomon Asks for Wisdom

Topic: Learning

Scripture: 1 Kings 2:1-4; 3:3-28

Simple Supplies: You'll need a backpack, Bible, and school supplies. Place the Bible in the backpack, then fill it with school supplies, such as a packet of pencils, an eraser, and a book.

Ask:

- **How many of you go to school?** Pause for kids to raise their hands.
- **How many of you have a brother or sister who goes to school?** Pause.
- **How many of you will go to school some day?**

By this time every child should have raised his or her hand. Say: **I've brought a backpack similar to ones that school children use to carry supplies. Let's see what's inside.** One at a time bring out each item and ask the following question. Pull out the Bible last. Remember to hold the items high so everyone can see. Ask:

- **How does this item help us learn?**

Say: **We can use pencils for writing or drawing; we can use an eraser when we make mistakes. We read from books to help us learn. All of these items help us learn lots!** Hold up the Bible, then open it to 1 Kings 3. **The *Bible* helps us learn how to live each day. Let's learn what the Bible tells us about King Solomon. God asked Solomon, "Ask for whatever you want me to give you." Solomon asked God to help him be wise. Solomon wanted wisdom to be king and to know right from wrong so that he** could rule the people well. **I don't think I would've asked God for that!** Ask:

- **How do we learn right from wrong?**

Say: **We can learn right from wrong and gain wisdom by coming to church, listening to Christian adults, praying, and reading the Bible.** Include other things the children mentioned. **Let's pray together. Instead of folding your hands together, put your hands on your heads as we pray to show that you want to learn, just as Solomon wanted to learn.** Pause.

Pray: **Dear God, thank you for the Bible, church, and other Christians who help us learn to live each day. Help us always follow you. In Jesus' name, amen.**

> **Cute Quote!** One little girl came up during the children's message time. She whispered to the leader, "My mom told me she'd give me a dollar if I don't talk during the children's message."

Elijah Helps a Widow

Topic: God's Care

Scripture: 1 Kings 17:7-24

Simple Supplies: You'll need a Bible, a see-through jar of flour, a see-through jar of oil, a paper plate, crackers, and a large plate. Place three crackers on the paper plate, then fill a large plate with the other crackers (enough so each child gets at least one).

Open your Bible to 1 Kings 17, and show the children the words. Say: **The Bible tells about a poor woman who had only enough flour** (hold up the jar of flour) **and oil** (hold up the jar of oil) **to make one last meal for herself and her son. She was sad, because she thought once they ate that little bit of food, they would die because they had nothing left. God sent Elijah to help her. Elijah** told her to use her tiny bit of flour and oil to make bread for the three of them! Elijah told her not to be afraid, because God would take care of them.

Set the jars to one side. Say: **The woman trusted God and shared her little bit of food. She made enough for Elijah, her son, and herself.** Set out the paper plate with three crackers on it. **She thought she had used up all of her flour and oil. But you know what? God kept the jars full. The flour and oil never ran out! Because she trusted God, she had enough flour and oil to make food for a long time.** Bring out the plate of crackers, and serve everyone. As they eat, ask:

• **How do you think the woman felt when God took care of her?**
• **How does God care for you?**

Say: **God cared for the woman and her son. He sent Elijah to give them hope. God gave them flour and oil so they could have food for a long time. God cares for us by giving us families, food, and friends.** Mention other things that kids shared. Pray: **Oh God, you are so good. You took such good care of the woman and her son, and I know you take care of me. Thank you for all the ways you have provided for my care. Help me to remember to thank everyone who cares for me. In Jesus' name, amen.**

Elijah Challenges the Prophets of Baal

Topic: One True God

Scripture: 1 Kings 18:16-40

Simple Supplies: You'll need a Bible.

Open your Bible to 1 Kings 18, and show the children the words. Say: **Today's Bible story is about the prophet Elijah. A prophet is a person who tells people messages from God.**

Elijah knew there was one true God. Hold up one finger and point up high on each word—"one," "true," and "God." Have the children repeat the motion and the phrase. **But many people in the land where Elijah lived weren't sure if they should follow the one true God** (have kids point up and repeat the phrase "one true God") **or if they should worship other gods. You and I know that this is silly. There are no other gods. There's only one true God!** Have kids point up and repeat the phrase. **There were 850 prophets who believed in fake gods with strange names like Baal. There was only one prophet, Elijah, who believed in the one true God!** Have kids point up and repeat the phrase. **The time came for Elijah to prove that the Lord was the one true God!** Have kids point up and repeat the phrase. **Baal's prophets built an altar, and Elijah built an altar. An altar was made of wood and sticks, and it was a special place for people to make sacrifices to God.**

Finally the altars were finished. Elijah told the prophets of Baal to go first, and to ask Baal to send fire to light their altar.

So the false prophets prayed to Baal. What happened? Nothing! Then they danced. What happened? Nothing!

Then they shouted and yelled. What happened? Nothing!

It was because their gods were fake! They were about to learn about our one true God! Have kids point up and repeat the phrase. **Elijah dug a hole around the altar. Then he had lots of water poured all over the wood. Not once, but three times! Whoosh! Whoosh! Whoosh! There was so much water, it poured all around the altar and into the hole he had dug! Then Elijah quietly prayed, "Answer me, O Lord, so these people will know that you are our one true God."** Have kids point up and repeat the phrase.

You know what happened? God sent fire! Yes! There was so much fire that it burned up the altar and all that water! Wow! When the people saw this they believed in our one true God. Point up and repeat the phrase "one true God." Ask:

• **Who can you tell about our one true God?**

As you close in prayer, have the children point up with one finger. Pray: **Dear God, I am so glad that I know you, our one true God. It is sad that there are so many other people who do not yet know that you are our one true God. Show me who I can tell** about you, and give me the courage to share how wonderful and powerful you are. In Jesus' name, amen.

Elisha Helps a Widow and Her Sons

Topic: God's Care

Scripture: 2 Kings 4:1-7

Simple Supplies: You'll need a Bible, ten paper cups, two identical pitchers, water, and a trash can. Place a little bit of water in one pitcher. Then fill the ten paper cups with water and pour that water into an identical pitcher. Place the full pitcher out of sight. Set out a trash can and the ten empty paper cups. (Depending on the size of the pitcher, you may need to use more cups of water so the pitcher is full.)

LEADER TIP

If you are working with a smaller number of children, give each child a cup, and as you fill each cup, have the children pour the water into another container of some sort. Continue filling the cups as often as needed until the pitcher is empty.

Open your Bible to 2 Kings 4. Say: **The Bible tells about a woman whose husband had died, and now people were coming to collect money he owed them. In Bible times someone who owed money might have to pay by giving up a child to be a slave or a servant! Ahh! The woman had sons, and she was afraid that the people who wanted her to pay the debts would take her sons! The woman told her problems to a man of God named Elisha.**

God wanted Elisha to help the woman so she wouldn't lose her sons. The woman had just a little oil. Hold up the pitcher with just a tiny bit of water in it. Show the children the water in the pitcher. **Elisha told her to ask her neighbors**

for empty jars—as many jars as she possibly could find. Choose one child to pass out ten empty cups to ten kids, and have those kids stand. While that is happening, switch the pitchers so you now have the full pitcher.

Elisha told her to pour the little oil she had into the jars. She did that and the jars filled with oil. She kept saying, "Bring me another one," and she kept pouring oil into all the jars she had gathered until each one was full. Keep saying, "Bring me another one" until you have filled all ten cups with water. Fill the cups over the trash can to catch any spills.

Each jar became full of oil, until every jar was filled, because God took the little bit of oil and turned it into lots of oil. It was a miracle! Have the kids say, "It was a miracle!" **Then Elisha told her to sell the jars of oil and pay off her debts! The woman and her sons would be OK!** Ask:

- **What would you be thinking or feeling if you were the woman or one of her sons?**
- **How does God show he cares for you?**

Say: **God sent Elisha to show the woman that he cared for her and her sons. God performed a miracle to provide for the woman and her sons—a miracle of lots of oil! The woman sold the oil and was able to pay her husband's debts. She and her sons would be OK. Don't we have an amazing God?**

Collect the cups of water from the children, and ask all of the children to hold their hands out in front of them like a cup. Pray: **Dear God, you truly are amazing. You cared for the woman and her sons in such a surprising way. You care for me, too, in amazing ways. Thanks so much for your love and care. In Jesus' name, amen.**

God Heals Naaman

Topic: Following God

Scripture: 2 Kings 5:1-16

Simple Supplies: You'll need a Bible and mini sticky notes or dots.

Ask:

• **When you're sick, how do your parents help you feel better?**

Say: **Our parents might hug us, fix us soup, or give us vitamins and medicine.** Add other ideas the kids mentioned. **In Bible times there were some sicknesses you could never get over. One of those sicknesses was leprosy. People who got leprosy suffered from horrible sores on their bodies, and eventually they would die. Because the disease could pass from one person to another, people who had leprosy had to go away from everyone they knew and live by themselves.** Pass out the sticky notes, and have the kids stick several on their hands and arms.

Open your Bible to 2 Kings 5, and show the children the words. Say: **The Bible tells about a mighty army commander named Naaman who had leprosy. Although Naaman was a powerful soldier, he didn't have enough power to heal himself of leprosy. One of Naaman's young servant girls told him about a prophet of God named Elisha. God had used Elisha to do many miracles, and now God wanted to use Elisha to heal Naaman.**

Naaman had to travel a long way to reach Elisha. Elisha told Naaman that God wanted him to wash seven times in the Jordan River. At first Naaman thought that was not good enough for him, an important army commander, and he didn't want to follow God's direction. He finally did after some of his men convinced him.

Let's pretend we're going with Naaman to the Jordan River. Have kids march in place. **OK, now we have to wash seven times!** Have kids bend their knees like they're dipping in a river and count "one," then stand up and bend and count "two," and so forth, all the way to "six." **We're coming to the seventh dipping! When you dip down this time, take off your sticky notes!** Have kids bend, take off their notes, then stand up "clean"! Ask:

- **How do you think Naaman felt when he came out of the water the seventh time and saw he had been healed?**
- **How did Naaman follow God in the story?**
- **How can we follow God today?**

Say: **Because Naaman followed God's direction, he was healed! The Bible says his skin was clean like that of a young boy! We can follow God by being kind to others, by bringing others to church, by learning about Jesus, and by living like Jesus every day.**

Tell the children they may keep the sticky notes or dots, and then close by praying: **Thank you, God, for the example of Naaman. He obeyed you even when it seemed a strange thing to do. Help me to follow you by learning more and more about you each day. In Jesus' name, amen.**

Jehoshaphat Trusts God for Victory

Topic: Trusting God

Scripture: 2 Chronicles 20:1-30

Simple Supplies: You'll need a Bible.

Ask:

- **What does it mean to trust someone?**
- **Who do you trust?**

Say: *Trust* **means to have faith that things will work out when we're worried. We can trust our parents, guardians, teachers, and** [include others the children mentioned]. **We can trust a lot of** people, and we can always trust God. **Right now, I need a volunteer. Someone who trusts me!** Pick a volunteer, and have him or her stand. [Name of child], **turn your back to me and cross your arms over your chest.** Wait for the volunteer to do this. **When I say, "Trust me," lean back into my arms, and trust me to catch you!** Before you try this, make a big deal out of it by saying, "Do you kids trust me to catch our volunteer?" "Do the adults out there trust me to catch our volunteer?" Then catch the volunteer three times, having the volunteer fall back a bit farther each time.

Afterward ask:

- [Name of child], **was it easy or hard for you to trust me? Why?**
- **Did the rest of you trust me to catch our volunteer? Why?**

Open your Bible to 2 Chronicles 20, and show the children the words. Say: **We trust people who love us and want the best for us. The Bible tells about King Jehoshaphat, who trusted God. The king knew God loved him and wanted the best for his people. Well, one day the king heard that a huge army of enemies was coming to fight them. King Jehoshaphat was afraid, because he knew they didn't have many people to fight back! The king did the right thing. He prayed, and he asked his people to pray to God and ask God what to do.** Have the kids fold their hands in prayer. **God told the people to trust him to help them. The people were so happy that they praised God!** Have the kids wave their hands in the air. **The next day, when Jehoshaphat and the people went out to meet the enemies, they continued to sing and praise God. God confused the enemies, and they began fighting among themselves! Jehoshaphat's people didn't even have to fight against their enemies. God won the battle for them. We can always trust God to help us.**

LEADER

At the end of the children's message, be like King Jehoshaphat and the people and sing a praise song such as "Our God Is So Great!" or "Great and Mighty Is He."

Close by praying: **Dear God, please hear us as we silently tell you something we're afraid of.** Pause. **Help us always trust you to help us. We know you love us and want the best for us. In Jesus' name, amen.**

 **Cute Quote!** When asked if she'd like to sing a hymn, three-year-old Maddie replied, "No, I'd rather sing a her."

The Humongous Book of Children's Messages

Josiah Discovers God's Word

Topic: God's Laws

Scripture: 2 Chronicles 34:1-33

Simple Supplies: You'll need a Bible and small squares of paper rolled up tightly like scrolls and held closed with rubber bands. Hide the Bible close to where you'll be gathered for the children's message.

Ask:

- **Have you ever lost something then found it again? What was it?**
- **How did you feel when you found it?**

LEADER

If you have lots of Bibles in the meeting area, choose a Bible that is distinctive from the rest, such as a big red one or a Bible that has a blue leather cover.

Tell about a time you lost something then found it. Say: **When I found something I lost, I was so thankful because it meant so much to me. I know there is a special Bible in this room, and I need help finding it.** Describe the Bible you want the children to find. **When I say "go," help me find it. Ready? Go!** When someone finds the Bible, gather the kids again. Congratulate all the children for helping you find something that means so much to you. Open the Bible to 2 Chronicles 34, and show the children the words. Say:

The Bible tells about King Josiah who was a leader of God's people. He had been king since he was eight years old! Let the kids say how old they are. **Just being a kid at eight years old takes a lot of work! Just think how much work an eight-year-old king would have to do! Josiah was a good king who loved God. When Josiah got older, he was having their Temple repaired. The Temple was like a big church. While they were fixing it up, they found something that had been missing for a long time—God's laws!** Hold up the Bible. **At that time the Bible was not in a book form like we have now, but was written on scrolls.** Ask:

- **Does anyone know what a scroll is?**

Say: **The Bible that the people found when they were repairing the Temple was the part of the Bible that includes the Ten Commandments.** Ask:

- **How do you think they felt when they found God's laws?**
- **What do the commandments teach us?**

Say: **They were so thankful to find something that had been lost a long time. The commandments tell us how God wants us to live. When King Josiah heard God's laws, he was so sad because he knew the people weren't living like God wanted them to. King Josiah helped the people. He read God's laws to them and helped them follow God.** Read 2 Chronicles 34:33b: **"As long as he lived, they did not fail to follow the Lord, the God of their fathers."**

Hand each child one of the rolled up squares of paper. Close by praying: **Dear God, help us read your Word and listen to stories about you. Give us courage to tell our friends about you too. Thanks for the Bible, which shows us how to live. In Jesus' name, amen.**

Nehemiah Rebuilds the Wall

Topics: Prayer, God's Protection

Scripture: Nehemiah 2:11–6:19

Simple Supplies: You'll need a Bible, chairs, newsprint, and several paper wads.

Gather the children around the Bible that you have opened to Nehemiah 2. Say: **The Bible tells about Nehemiah, who served a king in a different country from his own. Nehemiah was sad because he heard the walls of his home city—Jerusalem—were just a pile of rubble and stone. Without good walls for protection, Jerusalem would be in danger from its enemies. Nehemiah** prayed to God and asked for direction. **God guided him to tell the king. When the king heard the news, he told Nehemiah to go home and rebuild the walls.**

Nehemiah got the people together to build the walls. But enemies were making fun of the builders and threatening to hurt them, so Nehemiah had to divide the workers in half—one group would build while the other group protected them. Throughout the whole time, Nehemiah prayed when he faced tough times. **Let's pretend these chairs are the materials we need to build a wall. When I give the signal, half of you will be the builders and arrange these chairs in a row like a wall.** Motion to half of the kids. **The other half of you will be the protectors.** Motion to the other half. **Stand in front of the builders, and use these sheets of newsprint as shields.** Hand out the sheets of newsprint. **Ready? Build!** Toss wadded sheets of paper at the shields while the builders build the wall. After the wall is built, collect the shields and paper wads, and set them aside. Ask:

- **What was it like to build while paper wads were coming at you?**
- **What was it like to protect the builders?**
- **How does God protect us in our lives?**

Say: **It must have been scary to be rebuilding the walls of Jerusalem and facing enemies at the same time. Throughout everything, Nehemiah prayed. God protected everyone who was building the wall and helped them finish it. No matter what we face in life, we can be like Nehemiah and pray to God for help and protection.**

Have the children stand and link arms together to form a wall. Then lead the children in prayer. **Dear God, sometimes we have hard jobs to do, but I am so glad that you protect us. Help us be better pray-ers, like Nehemiah was. I thank you that you hear my prayers and protect me. In Jesus' name, amen.**

Queen Esther Is Brave (1)

Topic: Courage

Scripture: Esther 1–5; 8–9

Simple Supplies: You'll need a Bible and a trophy (or a medal).

Say: **Today we're going to talk about being brave—or having courage.** Open your Bible to Esther, and show the children the words. **The Bible tells about Queen Esther who was very brave and stood up for her people. The king had an advisor who hated Queen Esther's people and wanted them all killed. Esther had anything she could ever want, but she knew that if she *didn't* say something, her family and all their friends would be killed. But if she *did* say something, the king might get mad and not have her as his queen anymore. He might even have *her* killed! She was in a tough spot and could have decided not to risk her life. But Esther was brave. She went to the king and stood up for her people. The king changed his mind and her people were saved.** Ask:

- **Why did it take courage and bravery for Esther to go to the king?**

Say: **Queen Esther had courage! She was brave! She risked everything, even her life, to do what was right.** Hold up the trophy and say: **Today, when we do brave things like win races or do our best at school, we might get a trophy. I'm going to ask a question. If you have an answer, hold the trophy while you say it.** Ask:

- **When have you needed to be brave and have courage?**

As kids answer, have them hold the trophy then pass it on. Some answers might be "Standing up to a bully," "Helping my little sister not cry during a storm but I was scared myself," or "Moving to a new school." When everyone is finished, hold the trophy.

Say: **God helped Queen Esther have courage, and God helps us, too.** Pass the trophy around, and have kids say, "Dear God, help me have courage like Queen Esther." End by praying: **We pray in the** name of your courageous Son, Jesus, who gave his life so we could live forever. In Jesus' name, amen.

Queen Esther Is Brave (2)

Topic: Courage

Scripture: Esther 1–5; 8–9

Simple Supplies: You'll need a Bible, toy or paper crown, bright-colored blanket or towel to use as a royal cape, and a stick or baton to use as a scepter.

Open your Bible to Esther, and show kids the words. Say: **Today we'll learn about Queen Esther. But first, I need someone who will pretend to be this lovely lady.** Choose one child to be Queen Esther. **Queen Esther was married to a king.** Place the crown on her head. **She probably had lots of money, so she probably had cool clothes.** Place the cape around her shoulders. **Because she was queen, she could tell people what to do!** Give the child the stick or baton to use as a scepter. **My! What a lovely Queen Esther.**

Let's play a game called "Queen or King for a Minute." You're a queen, so you have power to tell us what to do! We'll do it. Guide the queen in saying things like, "Pat someone's back," "Give a hug," or "Go to someone and tell them they look nice." Encourage kids to follow orders, then switch. Let another child be queen or king and give some orders.

Say: **Good job giving orders, kings and queens. Well, in our story, Queen Esther had anything she wanted in the whole world, but there were other people who worked for the king who hated her and her friends and family. These bad people wanted all of Esther's people killed. Esther bravely went to the king and stood up for her people. The king could have kicked her out of the** palace, or even killed her, but he listened to her and changed his mind. Queen Esther used her power and saved her people. Ask:

- **Why do you think Queen Esther used her power for good?**
- **How can we have courage like Queen Esther?**

Say: **Queen Esther used her power and saved her people. We can always be brave and do the right thing like her. If we see someone being picked on, we can stick up for the person. When we see someone who seems lonely, we can go and talk to the person. There are all kinds of ways we can have courage like Queen Esther.**

Tell the children to think of one way that they might need to be brave and have courage. Hold the scepter and point to each child. Say: **Dear God, please help** [child's name] **be courageous when...**(pause for the child to tell when they might need courage). End the prayer: **In Jesus' name, amen.**

 The topic of a children's message was "boldness" or "courage." When the leader asked, "What does the word *boldness* mean?" one child responded, "It's a person with no hair on his head."

The Lord Is My Shepherd

Topic: Service

Scripture: Psalm 23

Simple Supplies: You'll need a Bible, scissors, paper punch, yarn, and copies of the "Sheep Dog Dog Tag" (p. 83). Photocopy, cut out, then hole punch the dog tags (one per child). Loop yarn through the holes so kids can wear them.

Ask:

- **How many of you love dogs?**
- **How do dogs show us they're our friends?**

Sheep Dog
Dog Tag

The Lord
is my shepherd;
I'm a good
sheep dog
to others.

Permission to photocopy this page from *The Humongous Book of Children's Messages* granted for local church use. Copyright © Group Publishing, Inc., P.O. Box 481, Loveland, CO 80539. www.grouppublishing.com

LEADER

Make the dog tags more durable by laminating them or by covering them with clear shelf paper.

Say: **One of the neat things that some dogs do is help out on farms and ranches. Lots of times farmers rely on dogs to watch the animals, to protect the animals, to lead them to food and water, and to keep them on the right path so they don't get into trouble.** Open your Bible to Psalm 23, and show the children the words. **Listen to Psalm 23 that talks about a special type of farmer, a shepherd, and the sorts of things he does to take care of a flock of sheep. Hmm. I wonder if this shepherd had a sheep dog along with him.** Read Psalm 23, then say: **A pastor once said, "Jesus is my shepherd and we are his flock of sheep. But sometimes when thinking of my job as a Christian, I like to think of myself as a sheep dog. I love Jesus no matter what. I'm loyal. I work with Jesus guiding the flock."** Ask:

- **How can we be like good sheep dogs and help our shepherd, Jesus, do his work?**
- **Who can you tell about Jesus and bring into the flock?**

Say: **Let's be good sheep dogs and work with Jesus our shepherd. Let's tell everyone about Jesus, because we love Jesus so much.**

As a closing prayer, place a dog tag over each child's head and say: **Dear Jesus, help** [name of child] **be a loyal, loving worker for you.** After all children are wearing their dog tags, close by praying: **In Jesus the good shepherd's precious name, amen.**

Isaiah Sees God's Holiness

Topics: Worship, Forgiveness

Scripture: Isaiah 6:1-8

Simple Supplies: You'll need a Bible, a white sheet, a chair, and some hot cinnamon candies.

Open your Bible to Isaiah 6:1-8, and show the children the words. Say: **The Bible tells about a prophet of God named Isaiah who saw God in a vision—which is a special picture God gives people that they see with their minds. Isaiah saw the Lord seated on a throne. Let's use this chair to be the throne.** Motion to a chair. **The Bible also says that God's throne was high and exalted. So let's set it up higher. Exalted means it was above every other throne, more important and more powerful.** Place the chair somewhere higher, like on a platform or stage. **The train of God's robe filled the temple. That's like saying God was wearing a cape that covered all the floor of this room. That's a really big cape!** Unfold the white sheet and have some children help you wave it up and down and all around. Then drape it over the chair. **Above God were seraphs, which are a type of angel. Each seraph had six wings: two wings covered their faces, two wings covered their feet, and two wings helped them fly. Let's make a seraph.**

LEADER

Make as many seraphs as you can with the kids you have. If you need more, invite others in the room who may be watching to join in the fun.

Choose a volunteer and say: **Sit on the floor and cover your feet with your hands.** Choose another volunteer. **Kneel behind the first volunteer and flap your arms like wings.** Choose a third volunteer. **Stand behind the other two volunteers and cover your eyes. Wow. What a good seraph. The seraphs were saying over and over, "Holy, holy, holy!"** Ask:

- **What do you think** *holy* **means?**
- **What things about God make him holy?**

Direct the children who have formed a seraph to say, "Holy, holy, holy." Say: **Go ahead and repeat it over and over.** Encourage everyone to repeat this for about thirty seconds. **Good job! Everybody sit down again.** Ask:

- **How do you think Isaiah felt when he saw and heard about God's holiness?**
- **What would you have done?**

Say: **God is** *holy.* **That means he's perfect, powerful, without sin, not guilty of any bad thing, and worthy of our worship. It might be kind of hard to stand in front of God, who's so perfect, when we're not. Isaiah was afraid because of that. He told God he was a sinner, just as everyone is, and did bad things sometimes. We all do bad things sometimes and need to tell God. Let's** do that now. **Dear God, please hear us as we silently tell you something we're sorry for.** Pause for kids to pray. **One of the seraphs in the story flew to Isaiah and put a hot coal to his lips.** Pass out the hot cinnamon candies. **The angel told Isaiah that his sin was forgiven. Jesus forgives you when you ask for it! Isaiah was so happy that he told God he wanted to go out and tell people all about God. Let's tell everyone about our awesome, holy God who loves us and forgives us! Let's pray and tell God how we feel.**

Pray: **Dear God, I am amazed at how holy you are. And I know that I sin just like Isaiah sometimes. It is wonderful that you made a way to take away our sins through the death of Jesus. That is so wonderful that I want to tell other people about it. Help me always remember that you are holy and that you forgive us. In Jesus' name, amen.**

God Tells People to Get Ready

Topic: Salvation

Scripture: Isaiah 9:6; Jeremiah 33:14-16

Simple Supplies: You'll need a Bible, baby pictures, and copies of the birth announcement on page 87, one for each child and one you have filled in about yourself.

Gather the children, and show them the baby pictures. Say: **Aren't these baby pictures cute? God sure knows how to make cute people! When families give birth to or adopt babies, they sometimes send out birth announcements. They want to spread their joy at the miracle that's entered their homes!** Show the children the birth announcement. **See here? A birth announcement usually has the name of the baby, whether it's a boy or girl, the date and time of birth, height, and weight. I have filled in all that**

Newest Family Member

Please join us in welcoming the new arrival into our family!

Name _____

Boy or Girl _____

Birth Date and Time _____

Weight _____

Height _____

Permission to photocopy this page from *The Humongous Book of Children's Messages* granted for local church use. Copyright © Group Publishing, Inc., P.O. Box 481, Loveland, CO 80539.
www.grouppublishing.com

Messages for Old Testament Stories

information about me! Read the information on the announcement to the kids.

Open your Bible to Isaiah 9:6, and say: **The Bible had an announcement that told about a birth** *before* **the baby was born. God wanted people to get ready! Jesus was going to be born! Jesus the Savior of all people!** Ask:

- **Why was Jesus born?**
- **Who can we tell about Jesus?**

Say: **Jesus was born to save all people. A long time before Jesus was born, God told people Jesus was coming. God wants all people to be ready to love Jesus. God wants one big family in heaven with him, living forever!**

Give each child a birth announcement. Tell them: **Ask someone to help you fill in all this information about your birth. Put it on the refrigerator or in your room to help you remember the announcement about Jesus. You could talk about it with your friends and tell them about Jesus and why his birth was so special.**

Pray: **Dear God, thank you for getting us ready for Jesus. Help us tell people about Jesus so they can live forever too. In Jesus' name, amen.**

A leader asked, "What's the special time before Christmas when we get ready for Jesus' birth?" The leader was looking for the word *Advent*, but got a surprise instead when five-year-old Brandon eagerly raised his hand and exclaimed, "I know! It's Advil!"

Daniel in the Lions' Den

Topic: Courage

Scripture: Daniel 6:1-23

Simple Supplies: You'll need a Bible, and an elastic hair tie for each child. Ask a volunteer to use the hair ties to "close" the lions' mouths at the appropriate time in the story.

Open your Bible to Daniel 6:1-23, and show kids the words. Say: **Once there was a man named Daniel, who was a talented worker for a king. It soon became obvious that Daniel was the best worker of all. Daniel's co-workers were jealous of him. Let's all be a part of this story.**

Choose a child to be Daniel, and have him wave to everyone. Ask two others to be the jealous co-workers—ask them to fold their arms, scowl, and look jealous. Then choose another child to be the king. Position them across the front of the message area. Say: **The rest of us will be lions in the story. When it gets to our part, make your hands look like claws and teeth. Put them by your mouths and open and shut them.** Practice the action with the children.

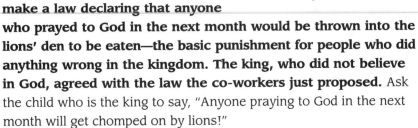

OK, on with our story. As I was saying, some of Daniel's co-workers were jealous of Daniel. They knew Daniel loved God, so the co-workers walked over to the king. Move your mouths and your hands, co-workers, like you're talking to the king. The co-workers told the king that he should make a law declaring that anyone who prayed to God in the next month would be thrown into the lions' den to be eaten—the basic punishment for people who did anything wrong in the kingdom. The king, who did not believe in God, agreed with the law the co-workers just proposed. Ask the child who is the king to say, "Anyone praying to God in the next month will get chomped on by lions!"

Daniel heard the decree, but being a person who believed in God, still got on his knees and prayed in his room in front of a window. Have the child who is Daniel kneel to pray.

His co-workers watched Daniel because they knew he loved God and wouldn't stop praying, and they did find him praying. Have the children who are the co-workers put their hands over their eyes as if looking for something. They should show pleasure that their plan has succeeded when they see "Daniel" praying.

The co-workers grabbed Daniel, and brought him to the king. They said, "We caught Daniel praying!" Have the children act this out.

Even though the king thought Daniel was a great guy, he realized he had to follow through with the punishment. The king told

the co-workers to put Daniel in with the lions for the night. OK "lions," let's make claw teeth and growl. Have the "co-workers" put Daniel in the middle of all the lions.

The king was very sad, because he liked Daniel and knew he was a very good man. Have the king look sad.

The co-workers were happy, because they thought they had gotten rid of Daniel. Have the children act this out.

The king couldn't sleep all night, because he was so upset and worried about Daniel.

Explain to the co-workers that they should join the lions, because their part in the story is over.

Say: **The lions paced in a circle around Daniel, snapping their mouths open and shut and roaring.** Have the children who are being lions walk around Daniel, pretending to roar. **But God sent an angel who shut the mouths of the lions!** Ask your volunteer to loosely wrap a hair tie around the hands of each of the children, so their "mouths" are shut.

The frustrated lions had to lie down and go to sleep, since they couldn't do anything else.

The very first thing in the morning, the king walked to the lions' den. The king was so surprised because Daniel was alive. Have the "king" do this.

Daniel explained to the king, "God kept me safe in the lions' den."

Have the king and Daniel hug or high five, and ask the lions to take off their hair ties and hold them. Ask:

- **How did God protect Daniel in the lions' den?**
- **How does God protect us?**

Say: **Daniel kept his faith, and God protected him by closing the lions' mouths! God protects us each day with guardian angels and families to surround us. Let's always keep our faith, just like Daniel. God protects us!**

Ask the kids to put the hair ties in a pile. As they do, have them say one thing they want God to protect them from, such as a bully at school, fear of failing a test, or any worry they have. Also include children who don't have hair ties.

Close by praying: **God, thanks for showing us how you protected Daniel. Thanks for protecting us from all the things that are problems in our lives. In Jesus' name, amen.**

Jonah Learns to Obey God

Topic: Obeying God

Scripture: Jonah 1–4

Simple Supplies: You'll need a Bible and tuna in a resealable plastic bag or bowl.

Ask the children:

- **What are some rules or chores your parents expect you to do?** Ideas could be "Be nice to my brother," "Clean my room," or "Do my homework."
- **What happens if you don't do what your parents want you to do?**

Say: **We might get grounded or get a timeout if we disobey our parents.** Ask:

- **What if we disobeyed our parents and the consequence was that all we could smell was fish?** Pass around the plastic bag or bowl of tuna, and invite kids to take a sniff.

Say: **That's what happened to a man named Jonah in our Bible story!** Open your Bible to Jonah, and show the children the words. **God wanted Jonah to go to a big, big city named Nineveh. The people there did not know about God and were not following God's ways. In fact, they were not being nice at all. They were very bad! God wanted Jonah to tell the people to stop being bad.** Ask:

- **Who knows what Jonah did? Did he go to Nineveh?**
- **What happened when Jonah took a boat the opposite way from Nineveh?**

Say: **Jonah disobeyed and ended up in the belly of a big fish. Maybe it smelled a bit like that tuna inside that fish!**

While he was inside the fish, Jonah prayed and told God he was sorry. After three days and three nights, the big fish spit Jonah out, and Jonah went to Nineveh. Ask:

- **Why should we obey our parents?**
- **Why should we obey God?**

Say: **Our parents and people who care for us want us to grow up to be loving, caring, Christian adults. We obey them, and we learn how to live life. God wants us to be loving, caring, Christians too. God wants us to obey him, because he made us and knows what's best for our lives.**

Set the tuna on the floor, and have kids join hands around it. Have them pretend they are like Jonah, outside the big fish. Go around the circle and have each person pray: "Please help me obey you always."

Close by praying: **Thank you so very much for showing us how important it is to obey. You want good things for us, and we need to obey you because you know us best. Thank you that you care for us. In Jesus' name, amen."**

Messages for New Testament Stories

Wise Men Come to Worship Jesus

Topic: Honoring Jesus

Scripture: Matthew 2:1-12

Simple Supplies: You'll need a Bible; four shopping bags; a large bottle of perfume; something that is gold, such as a lamp; a large scented candle; and a mirror. Place each object in a separate shopping bag, and place the bags on top of a table.

Open your Bible to Matthew 2:1-12, and say: **Once upon a time, a long time ago, when Jesus was born, some very important men came to visit Jesus. They've been called wise men, kings, and Magi. For now, let's just call them the wise men. They saw a star in the sky and followed it for a long time, across many lands, all the way to the house where Jesus was. They were so happy when they saw Jesus and his mother, Mary, that they bowed down and they gave him gifts.** Ask:

- **If you wanted to give Jesus a gift, what would you give him?**
- **Where would you go shopping?**

Say: **Let's look in these shopping bags and see the kinds of gifts the wise men might have brought to Jesus.** Open the first bag, and bring out the gold object. **One of the gifts was gold. Wow! A gift fit for a king!** Open the second bag, and bring out the nice-smelling candle. **Another gift was frankincense. This was something that was burned in the Temple at that time to praise God. It was also very expensive.** Open the third bag, and bring out the bottle of perfume. **The third gift was myrrh. That's a fun word to say. Say it with me: Myrrh! Myrrh was a precious perfume that was given to kings.** Pause by the last shopping bag. **The Bible doesn't tell us what Jesus did with these gifts, but we do know that his family had to take a trip to Egypt to keep Jesus safe, and they might have used these gifts to pay for that trip.**

We don't have gifts of gold, frankincense, and myrrh to give Jesus, but I do have another shopping bag here. Inside of it is a gift that Jesus wants more than anything. It's a gift that we all can give him! Open the shopping bag, and bring out the mirror. Hold the mirror so kids can see their reflections. **Jesus loves us so much, we are the best presents we can give him. We can love Jesus, tell others about him, and live with him forever!**

Pass the mirror around, and let each child look into it. As a child holds it, say: **Jesus loves** [name of child].

Pray: **Dear God, I am so glad Jesus was born. I want to bring gifts to Jesus, too, just like the wise men did long ago. I don't have gifts like they gave, but I can give him all of me. Thank you for the gift of Jesus. In his name, amen.**

Jesus Teaches the Disciples How to Pray

Topic: Prayer

Scripture: Matthew 6:5-13

Simple Supplies: You'll need a Bible and chocolate in different forms such as candy bars, cookies, and Hershey's Kisses.

Say: **I have a few items here I'd like you to help me compare.** Go through the pile of chocolate one item at a time describing each one. Be sure to hold the various forms of chocolate so all can see. Ask:

• **Are these items the same or different?**
• **Is there any one of these items that's better than the other?**

Say: **While we might like chocolate candy bars more than a chocolate cookie, they are all made with the same ingredient— chocolate! That's kind of like prayer. There are different ways to** pray, but no matter which way we pray, it's still the same—a prayer! Ask:

- **What are some different ways you've seen people pray?**
- **Which way do you like to pray?**

Say: **I've prayed standing, sitting, kneeling, and even lying down on my bed! I've prayed silently and out loud. I've prayed while crying, and I've prayed while laughing. I've prayed outside in parks, and up in the mountains, and I've prayed inside all sorts of different buildings. I've prayed all kinds of different ways, yet they are still the same—prayer!** Note: Please revise this list to fit your own experience.

Open your Bible to Matthew 6:5-13, and show the children the words. Say: **Jesus taught his disciples about prayer. He said prayer is between us and God. It's our way to talk directly with our God who loves us so. God loves to hear our prayers.**

Tell children you'll be leading them in prayer and they can each stand, sit, or kneel as you pray aloud. They can pray with their eyes open or closed—it's up to each of them because there's no one "right" way to pray. When children have chosen, pray aloud:

Dear God, you are so loving and good. I want to enjoy you and talk with you. Thank you that you want to talk with me, and that you aren't worried about what shape my prayer is. Help me remember that I can talk with you about everything! In Jesus' name, amen.

Give each child a different type of chocolate, and say: **When you eat your chocolate, you can pray, "Thank you, God, for hearing all of my prayers, no matter what shape they come in."**

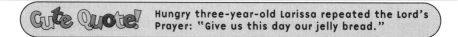 **Cute Quote!** Hungry three-year-old Larissa repeated the Lord's Prayer: "Give us this day our jelly bread."

Jesus Walks on Water

Topics: Keep Focused, Facing Fears

Scripture: Matthew 14:22-33

Simple Supplies: You'll need a Bible, a blue sheet, and two robes.

Open Your Bible to Matthew 14, and show the children the words. Say: **Today's Bible story is about Peter, one of Jesus' close friends, getting out of a boat and walking toward Jesus on the water. Let's act it out so we can see what this exciting event might have looked like.** Ask one child to be "Jesus" and another to be "Peter." Give them each a robe to wear. Spread out the blue sheet in front of them, and ask two kids to hold opposite ends. Ask the two kids to wiggle the sheet gently, close to the floor, so it looks like waves. Tell the rest of the kids that they are the disciples in the boat. Have Peter stay with the crowd until his cue to walk on the water. **Well, the disciples were in their boat rowing across a lake. They were rowing hard.** Have the children pretend to row a boat. **They're working very hard! The disciples looked across the water—it was stormy and dark, so they had to squint.** Have the children pretend to look across the water.

They saw someone walking on the water! The person was walking toward them. The disciples were extremely surprised! Have the children make a surprised face. **But they were also afraid because they thought they were seeing a ghost!** Have the children make a scared face and then say, "It's a ghost!"

But the person who was walking on the water in the storm was none other than Jesus himself. He yelled out to them, "Take courage! It is I. Don't be afraid." Have the child who is playing Jesus walk in the middle of the blue sheet as the children continue to make waves. Have him or her speak to the children.

So many surprises! First the disciples see someone actually walking on water, then they find out it is Jesus himself, and now they get another surprise. Peter, one of the disciples, stood up and said, "If it's you, tell me to come to you on the water!" Have the child you chose to be Peter stand up and say the words above. Ask:

- **What do you think the other disciples thought about what Peter said?**
- **What do you think you would have done if you were in the boat?**

Say: **But that was not all the surprises for the disciples. There is no way they thought Jesus would have Peter get out of the boat and into that water. But—surprise!—Jesus told Peter, "Come!"** Have Jesus tell Peter to come.

The disciples watched in amazement while Peter got out of the boat and started walking toward Jesus! At first Peter looked at Jesus while he was walking. Everything was going great. The disciples were even more surprised because Peter was actually walking on the water, just like Jesus. Have your Jesus and Peter act this out.

But then Peter started looking at the waves around him. The waves were getting bigger! And bigger! And the wind started blowing around him. Have everyone make noises like the wind and move the sheet up and down a little stronger.

Peter became so scared, because he had taken his eyes off of Jesus and he started to sink. Peter yelled out, "Lord save me!" Have your Peter start to kneel down and call out.

But Jesus immediately reached out and caught him. Jesus pulled Peter up, and both of them climbed into the boat. Have both children act out what you said.

Gather the robes and sheet, and applaud the actors and actresses. Ask:

- **Why did Peter start to sink?**
- **When have you been afraid?**
- **How can you stay focused on Jesus the next time you're afraid?**

Say: **Peter started to sink when he took his eyes off Jesus. We might face scary times like when a grandparent dies or when we have to go to a new school. But if we focus on Jesus, pray to him, and tell him our fears, he'll comfort us.**

Close by praying. **Dear God, please hear us as we silently tell you something we're afraid of.** Pause. **Help us keep our eyes on you and know that you will comfort us. You are always with us. Thanks for helping Peter, and thanks for helping us. In Jesus' name, amen.**

Jesus Enters Jerusalem

Topic: Honoring Each Other

Scripture: Matthew 21:1-11

Simple Supplies: You'll need a Bible and a red blanket or sheet.

Say: **Have you ever heard the phrase "Roll out the red carpet"? "Rolling out the red carpet" means to honor people with the best of everything! It means that you think the people are so special, like kings or queens, that they shouldn't even get dirt on their feet from walking. So I have this red blanket here, and I think you all are so special that I don't want you to get dirty as you listen to me, so here, let me roll this out for you to sit on. You won't all fit on my blanket, so some of you will have to sit on pretend blankets.** Put as many children as comfortable on your blanket and encourage other children to sit nearby. Open your Bible to Matthew 21:1-11, and show the children the words.

When Jesus was coming into Jerusalem, the people there knew he was very special. They wanted to treat him like a king. They didn't put blankets down for Jesus to walk on. They used their own clothes! Can you imagine that? It would be like you taking off your jacket so someone else could walk on it instead of the dirty ground. They wanted to honor Jesus with what they had, with part of themselves, so they used their clothes. Ask:

- **How can we show honor to Jesus?**
- **How can we show honor to others?**

Say: **We, too, can honor Jesus with what we have. When we share our toys, or give away clothes to people who don't have any, or give away food, or invite people into our homes, we are doing things that honor Jesus. When we give something to others, it is like "rolling out the red carpet" for them. It honors them, and it honors Jesus.** Ask:

- **When has someone shown honor to you?**
- **How do you feel when others show you honor?**

- **Of the ways you told me earlier about how to show others honor, what could you do today?**

Close by praying: **Dear Jesus, you truly are worthy of honor. You are so loving, so good, and so powerful. Help me know how to honor you and help me know how to treat others with honor. In your name I pray, amen.**

John Baptizes Jesus (1)

Topic: Baptism

Scripture: Mark 1:4-11

Simple Supplies: You'll need a Bible, a basin of water, and a towel.

Open your Bible to Mark 1:4-11, and show the children the words. Each time you say the word "baptism" or a variation of the word, take a handful of water from the bowl, lift it high, then let it trickle back into the bowl.

Say: **The Bible tells us about John who was Jesus' cousin. John was teaching people about God and *baptizing* a lot of people. He would tell people to tell God they were sorry for the bad things they did and to stop doing those things. We call that repenting. Then he'd *baptize* them in the Jordan River. The baptism was a picture of being washed clean of the bad things and a way of showing everyone that the person wanted to change the way he or she was living.**

One day Jesus came and asked John to *baptize* him. John knew that Jesus was the Son of God. What a day that must have been for John! John *baptized* Jesus in the Jordan. As Jesus was coming up out of the water he was *baptized* in, he saw God's Spirit descending on him like a dove, and a voice came from heaven saying, "You are my Son, whom I love; with you I am well pleased." What an awesome sight it would've been to see Jesus' *baptism*. Ask:

- **How did Jesus please God?**
- **How can we please God?**

Say: **We know that God loves us no matter what, and we don't have to earn that love. We can please him though! Jesus pleased God when he was baptized. God told everyone that Jesus was his Son. We can please God when we obey him, when we love our families, when we love others, and when we tell others about Jesus.**

LEADER

Adapt the message according to your church's view of baptism. If you use a baptismal font, gather the children by it for the message. If you baptize by immersion, gather the children near the baptistery.

Ask for volunteers to say a prayer. Whoever prays can cup his or her hand with water, and let it trickle back into the bowl. Wipe hands dry with the towel after each one prays. Close by praying: **Dear God, thank you for the work John did getting people ready for Jesus. I know that you love me just the way I am. I want to please you by the things I do and the way I live my life. In Jesus' name, amen.**

Tell kids to remember Jesus' baptism each time they hear trickling water this week—when the bathtub fills, when the sink fills, or when they shower.

John Baptizes Jesus (2)

Topic: God's Children

Scripture: Mark 1:4-11

Simple Supplies: You'll need a Bible and photocopies of the "Beloved Child" messages (p. 103) to give to several parents who will stand and read the words at the appropriate time in your message.

Open your Bible to Mark 1:4-11, and say: **When Jesus began his work of telling about God, he went to the Jordan River to be baptized by his cousin John. When Jesus came up out of the water, the most wonderful thing happened. The heavens split** apart and Jesus looked up to see God's Spirit like a dove coming down on him. Then he heard a wonderful message from God: "You are my Son, whom I love; with you I am well pleased." Ask:

- **How do you think Jesus felt when he heard those words?**
- **How do you feel when people tell you they love you?**
- **Who tells you they love you?**

Say: **God loved his Son, Jesus, and he loves us, too. God sent Jesus into this world for us. Because Jesus lived, died, and rose again, we can live forever in heaven! When our parents or guardians or friends tell us how special we are, maybe we can feel a little bit like Jesus felt when God told Jesus he was well pleased.**

[Name of child]**, can you hear how special you are?** That child's parent should stand and proclaim, "[Name of child], you are my beloved [son/daughter]. And I am very pleased with you." Do this with each of the people you gave the handout to before the children's message. After everyone has heard the affirmation, ask:

- **How did you feel when you heard those words?**

Say: **I know some of your parents aren't here, and there's not time for all your parents to talk, so let me say it for them. All of you are my beloved children. And I am very pleased with you.**

Turn and address the adults in the meeting. Say: **Parents and others, we need to remember how important it is to tell our kids how special they are and how much God loves them. When we do, God speaks his message of love through our words.**

Pray: **Oh, God. It is such good news that you love us so much. When things are hard and it seems like we aren't special to anyone, help us to remember that you love us so much you gave your only Son for us. Thank you for loving us that much. In the name of your only Son, Jesus, amen.**

LEADER

Be sensitive to the children whose parents aren't in the room during the message. Also, be aware of children who might have a guardian instead of a mom and dad.

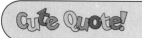 **Cute Quote!** Just prior to a baptism, a seven-year-old boy asked the leader, "How many people are being bath-tized today?"

Beloved Child

"

_____

[Name of child]

you are my beloved

_____.

[son/daughter]

And I am very

pleased with you."

Permission to photocopy this page from *The Humongous Book of Children's Messages* granted
for local church use. Copyright © Group Publishing, Inc., P.O. Box 481, Loveland, CO 80539.
www.grouppublishing.com

Jesus Calls His Disciples (1)

Topic: Following Jesus

Scripture: Mark 1:14-20

Simple Supplies: You'll need a Bible, a blanket, a stick, a five-foot piece of string, a clothespin, photocopies of the fish shape and the person shape (below). Fashion a fishing pole from the stick, the string, and the clothespin. Photocopy and then cut out the fish and person shapes. Photocopy enough people shapes so each child can have one. Ask three people to help you during the message.

Ask two of the volunteers to hold up the blanket so kids can't see behind it. Have the third volunteer get behind the blanket with the fish shape and the person shape. Tell the volunteer ahead of time that a child will be fishing with a clothespin. The first time, the volunteer clips on a fish. The second time, the volunteer clips on the person shape.

Open your Bible to Mark 1:14-20, and say: **The Bible tells us that when Jesus first began his ministry, he started calling people to follow him and help out. He wanted to teach these people about God's plan for all of us. Some of the people Jesus called were fishermen. Who'd like to show us what a fisherman does?** Give a child the fishing pole with the clothespin attached. Help the child throw the clothespin over the blanket to "fish." Tell the child to be sure to hang on to the pole. The volunteer will attach a fish, give the string a tug, then the child will "reel" in the catch. Ask the child to hold it high.

Look what our fisherman caught! A fish! Jesus told the fishermen to come and follow him, and he'd give them something else to catch. Watch. Ask the child to throw the clothespin over the blanket again. The volunteer will attach a person shape, give the string a tug, then the child will "reel" in the catch. Ask the child to hold it high.

Look what our fisherman caught! A person! Jesus told the fishermen that they would be fishers of men and women! Ask:

- **What do you think Jesus meant when he said that the disciples would catch people?**
- **How can we bring others to Jesus?**

Say: **Jesus wanted the disciples to follow him, and they'd help him catch people. The disciples would go where Jesus went, learn what Jesus wanted to teach them, and help other people know about Jesus.**

Give each child a person shape, and have them think about who they can tell about Jesus. Pray: **Dear God, thanks for calling the fishermen to help you fish for people. Help us tell others about you too. In Jesus' name, amen.** Ask the children to tape the person shape on the refrigerator or on their bathroom mirror to remind them to tell others about Jesus.

A leader was trying to get the point across that we are saved by God's grace through faith in Jesus. She asked, "If I sold my house and my car, had a big garage sale, and gave all my money to the church, would I get into heaven?"

"No!" the children answered.

"If I cleaned the church every day, mowed the yard, and kept everything neat and tidy, would I get into heaven?"

"No!" the children answered again.

"Well," the leader continued, "then how can I get into heaven?"

In the back of the crowd of kids, a five-year-old boy shouted, "You gotta be dead!"

Jesus Calls His Disciples (2)

Topic: Following Jesus

Scripture: Mark 1:14-20

Simple Supplies: You'll need a Bible and a box of fish-shaped crackers.

Say from the back of the room: **Hey, guys and gals! I'm not going to call you up for the children's message the way I usually do. Instead, I'm going to do what Jesus did a long time ago. As Jesus walked along, he would see people he knew would be good disciples, and he called them. They dropped everything and followed him.** Begin to walk into the crowd.

Let's see. There's [name of child]. **Follow me!** Motion with your hand. Continue calling all the kids who want to follow you. Toward the end of the march around the room, say: **The people Jesus called didn't know where he would lead them, but they trusted Jesus and followed him.** Bring the kids up front.

When you are a disciple, you follow Jesus your whole life. You have to make choices. For instance, maybe not all of your school friends go to church, so when you're at church you can't play with them. But the rewards of following Jesus are so great. Ask:

• **What good things do you get for following Jesus?**

Say: **One of the best things that I know is that when we follow Jesus our sins are forgiven and we get to live forever with him in heaven. That's awesome. I'm so glad I follow Jesus. Aren't you?**

You can read about Jesus gathering some of his disciples here, in the book of Mark. It's the second book in the New Testament part of your Bibles. Show children your Bible, open to Mark 1:14-20.

Say: **Jesus told some of his followers who were fishermen that they would quit catching fish and start catching men. That meant they'd be telling others about Jesus. We can tell others about Jesus, too, and these fishy snacks will be a reminder to be fishers for people!**

Hand out the fish-shaped crackers.

Close by praying: **Jesus, thank you that I can follow you. Help me be more like you and do all you want me to do. I know there are lots of people who don't know you and don't follow you. Help me tell them about you and how wonderful it is to follow you. In your name I pray, amen.**

Jesus Heals a Paralyzed Man (1)

Topic: Bringing Our Friends to Jesus

Scripture: Mark 2:1-12

Simple Supplies: You'll need a Bible and a beach towel or blanket.

Open your Bible to Mark 2:1-12, and say: **Our Bible story tells about a sick man who couldn't walk. He wanted to be healed! So his friends carried the man to Jesus on a mat. What good friends! Let's see what this might have been like.**

Lay the beach towel at one side of the message area. Ask a small child to lie down on it. Stand several feet away from the towel. Then ask two friends to take hold of two corners of the towel, and *slowly* pull the child to you. Tell the child on the towel to hang on! As the friends are pulling the towel, say: **The friends in the story wanted to bring the sick man to Jesus so Jesus could heal him. When they got to Jesus, he healed the man.** Have the child stand up and get off the towel. Let others try the same thing as time permits. Ask:

- **How did his friends help the sick man?**
- **How do you think the man felt when Jesus healed him?**
- **What friend can you tell about Jesus?**

Say: **Just like the friends in the story brought the man to Jesus, we can tell our friends about Jesus and bring them to church to learn about him. Jesus wants everyone to believe in him. So let's tell our friends.**

Ask the children to sit all around the towel so that everyone can touch it. Say: **As you touch this towel, picture in your mind someone you could bring to Jesus. If you can't think of anyone, ask God to help you meet someone who you could bring to Jesus.** Pause for a moment.

LEADER

If you think you will have a large group of children who will not all fit around a single towel, set out as many as you will need so that every child can touch a towel.

Dear God, thanks for friends. Thanks for showing us the example of the friends who brought the man to you. Thanks for healing the man. Please help us to bring our friends to church so they learn more about you. In Jesus' name, amen.

Encourage the kids to pray for their friends each time they touch a towel this week.

Jesus Heals a Paralyzed Man (2)

Topic: Helping Friends

Scripture: Mark 2:1-12

Simple Supplies: You'll need a Bible, a chair, and a bag of snacks. Place the chair at a spot to one side, and hold onto the bag of snacks.

Say: **Can I have a helper today? I need somebody who likes snacks. I have some snacks for you, but there is a problem and I'd like to see if you can solve it.** Choose a smaller child to be the helper, and have the person sit in the chair.

Here's the problem. I'm going to place these snacks way over here. Walk about twenty feet from the chair, and set down the bag of snacks. **I'd like to give you those snacks. Would you like the snacks?** Pause for the reaction. **Great! The only problem is that you can't leave the chair to get them. So how can you get the snacks?** Let all the kids shout out ways to get the snacks.

I'll give a hint. Open your Bible to Mark 2:1-12, and say: **It's in the book of Mark. Some people were trying to get their friend, who was a paralyzed man, to see Jesus. Being paralyzed means you can't walk. Here's the hint from the story. "Some men came, bringing to him a paralytic, carried by four of them."** Emphasize "carried by four of them." **Do you get the hint? Ah. Ask four friends to help!** Ask four strong kids to each grasp a different area of the chair and carry it over to the snacks. Encourage the child on the chair to wrap his or her arms around the friends as they lift. When they get to the bag, have them gently set down the chair, and have the volunteer pick up the snacks. Then have the volunteer give snacks to everyone. Ask:

- **How did the friends help in the story?**
- **How do our friends help us each day?**
- **How can we be good friends?**

Say: **The man in the story wouldn't have been able to get to Jesus if his friends didn't help. One of the greatest things we can do for our friends is to bring them to Jesus. Sometimes we need to be able to ask others for help. After all, that's what friends are for!**

Have each child find a partner. Tell partners to hold each other's arms near the elbow as if forming a seat to carry someone.

Say: **As you hold arms with your partner, think of someone you can help and be a good friend to.** Close in prayer: **Dear God, I am so glad you want us to be good friends. Please help me think of a way I can be a good friend this week. Show me how to help my friends learn more about you. In Jesus' name, amen.**

Jesus Calms the Storm

Topic: Facing Fears

Scripture: Mark 4:35-41

Simple Supplies: You'll need a Bible, and a blue streamer and a green streamer for each child.

Give each child a blue streamer for one hand and a green streamer for the other (about twelve inches long). Ask the children to hold their streamers and stand in a line across the front of the room.

Hold up your Bible, and say: **Today we're going to hear a story about Jesus calming a storm. Your job is to be the wild waves. Let's practice.** Ask the kids to crouch down. When you point from one end of the line to the other, have them stand, stretch their arms and streamers tall, then crouch back down. **Great job, waves! Well, in our story Jesus and his disciples got in a boat on a lake. Jesus was sleeping in the boat. At first the waves were small.** Motion to the kids to do a gentle wave. **Then the waves got bigger.** Motion to the kids for a bigger wave. **Finally, a big storm came, and the waves were huge!** Motion for the kids to do wave after wave, really high! **The disciples were afraid, and woke up Jesus. Jesus told the waves, "Quiet! Be still!"** Motion for the kids to stop immediately, and crouch as they were before.

Gather the kids, and ask:

• **Why were the disciples afraid?**
• **How did Jesus help?**
• **When are you sometimes afraid?**
• **How can Jesus help us?**

Say: **The disciples were very afraid of the wind and the waves. But Jesus stopped the storm and took care of them. When we're afraid, we can pray to Jesus and know that he hears us. Jesus will comfort us.**

Ask kids to think of a fear they want to give to Jesus. Ask them to stand across the room again. When they do their part of the wave, have them shout out a fear. Then have them crouch down again. Pray: **Jesus, we give you our fears. Thanks for calming us and caring for us always. In your name, amen.**

Jesus Blesses the Children

Topic: Trust

Scripture: Mark 10:13-16

Simple Supplies: You'll need a Bible. Ask three adults to help with this message. Ask them to act like children (see the message for ideas) and gather with the others when you ask them to.

Say: **OK, everyone gather around. It's time for the children's message!** Wait until everyone, young and old, gather around. **Welcome!** Open your Bible to Mark 10:13-16, and say: **Today we're going to hear a story about Jesus and some children. People were bringing little children to Jesus to have him touch them, but the disciples tried to keep them away. When Jesus saw this, he said, "Let the little children come to me...for the kingdom of God belongs to such as these...Anyone who will not receive the kingdom of God like a little child will never enter it." And he took the children in his arms, put his hands on them, and blessed them. Isn't that neat? Jesus wants us to be like children!** Ask:

- **What did you like most about the story?** Wait for responses, but have the adults act like little kids and answer "I wiked it a wot!" and "I tot it was cool!"

- **What do you think Jesus meant about being like a child?** Wait for responses; the adults should continue to act like little children.

Say: **These grown-ups are funny acting like kids!** Have the grown-ups say more silly things like, "We wove you!" **Sometimes it is fun to act like little babies. Can you do that?** Allow the children to pretend to be babies for just a brief time.

Jesus wasn't thinking about having grown-ups pretend to be little kids! Jesus wanted everyone to totally trust him just like a child trusts a grown-up who's loving and caring.

Close by praying: **Dear God, it is fun to be children. I am so glad that Jesus loved children. Help me remember that Jesus wants me to totally trust him. In his name, amen.**

 One leader ended her message about Jesus setting us free by saying, "Free at last; we are free at last!" One little girl responded, "Mrs. Rose, me not free. Me four!"

Jesus Heals the Blind Man

Topic: Faith

Scripture: Mark 10:46-52

Simple Supplies: You'll need a Bible and blindfolds (one for each pair of children). Place a few chairs around the room.

Form pairs, and give each pair a blindfold. Say: **Let's play a game called "Airplane." Choose which one of you will be the airplane and which one will be the air traffic controller who guides the airplane.** Pause while kids do this.

"Airplanes," you'll need guidance through a foggy night. So put on the blindfolds and pretend it's foggy—you can't see! Pause while partners help their airplanes put on their blindfolds. **Airplanes, your "air traffic controllers" will walk beside you and guide you around the room, using their voices only. Trust your air traffic controllers, and do what they say. They'll bring you through the fog to a safe landing!** Let the air traffic controllers talk their airplanes around the room, around chairs, then back to where they started. If you have time, let kids switch, so they experience both roles.

Afterward, ask:

- **What was it like to be the airplane?**
- **What was it like to be the air traffic controller?**

Open your Bible to Mark 10:46-52, and show the children the words. Say: **The Bible tells a story about a man who couldn't see. It was like he'd been wearing a blindfold for a long time. He was sitting by the roadside when he heard Jesus' voice! Kind of like how you listened for your air traffic controller's voice.**

The blind man knew help had arrived! When Jesus called to the blind man, people said: "Cheer up! On your feet! He's calling you!" The blind man listened and obeyed. He threw off his coat, jumped to his feet, and came to Jesus. The blind man had faith that Jesus could heal him. Jesus helped him see! Ask:

- **How did the blind man show faith?**
- **What makes our faith strong?**

Say: **The blind man had faith in Jesus. He heard his voice and knew he would help. He threw off his coat, jumped to his feet, and came to Jesus. We can make our faith strong by listening to Jesus' words in the Bible, at church, and with Christian friends.**

Have the children close their eyes while you pray: **Dear Jesus, when we can't see the way to go or what to do, help us have faith that you are here.** Ask the children open their eyes. **Thanks for the faith of the blind man you helped see. Thanks for giving us the friends and families we see now, the Bible, and our church that helps our faith grow strong. In Jesus' name, amen.**

Jesus Notices a Widow's Giving

Topic: Offering

Scripture: Mark 12:41-44

Simple Supplies: You'll need a Bible, two metal bowls, lots of coins, and a table.

Open your Bible to Mark 12:41-44, and show the children the words. Say: **The Bible tells us that one day Jesus and his disciples were in the Temple, which is like a church. Jesus was watching what people were doing with their offerings.** Motion to the table with the two metal bowls and coins. Set two coins aside.

There were lots of rich people who were giving huge amounts of money! Pour the coins into one bowl so kids can hear the rush of clinking. **Wow! Lots and lots of money!**

Then he noticed a poor widow, which means her husband had died. This poor widow gave her offering. Drop the two coins in the other metal bowl so kids hear "clink, clink." Ask:

- **Who do you think gave the most?**
- **How do you know?**

Say: **Jesus said the poor widow gave the most. The rich people gave out of their wealth. They had lots more money at home and only gave a little bit of what they had.** Shake the huge amount of coins around in one bowl.

The poor widow gave out of her poverty. She had nothing more at home. She gave everything she had to live on. Ask:

- **What did the widow do that Jesus thought was so neat?**
- **How can we be like the widow with our offering?**

LEADER TIP

You also could give kids two chocolate coins wrapped in gold foil. Encourage them to give their coins away, like the woman gave in the Bible story.

Say: **The rich people were giving just a small amount of their money. The widow gave everything to God. It showed she had trust that God would take care of her. We can give money in offering at church or at Sunday school, we can watch for kids at school who might be hungry and we can share our lunch. And we can share toys with children who don't have the toys we have.** Mention other ideas kids say.

Close in prayer: **God, I know that you want us to follow you with all that we are. Help us be like the widow who was happy to give to you even when it was the last she had. In Jesus' name, amen.**

Cute Quote! A pastor was giving a children's message. A young girl turned to the pastor's son and handed him a quarter. She whispered, "If I miss the offering, can you just give this to your dad?"

Jesus Grows Up

Topic: Spiritual Growth

Scripture: Luke 2:40

Simple Supplies: You'll need a Bible and a yardstick.

Ask everyone to crouch as low as he or she can. Say: **I wonder how tall you are now.** Go around the group and use the yardstick to measure their heights as they crouch. Then have the group "uncurl" a bit more as you measure some of them again. Then ask them to stretch tall as you measure a few more. **Wow! You sure grew a lot in the last minute or so!** Ask:

LEADER

Be sensitive to kids who are shorter or taller than the others. Don't call attention to their size, simply use the measuring stick as an introduction to the topic of growing up physically.

- **What do you need to grow up physically?**
- **What kinds of things can you do now?**
- **What kinds of things will you be able to do as you get bigger?**

Say: **We need good food, sleep, and exercise to grow up with strong bodies. As we grow, we can do more things like ride bikes, skateboard, and swim.** Add other ideas kids mentioned.

Open your Bible to Luke 2:40, and show the children the words. Say: **The Bible tells us a lot about Jesus when he was a baby and a lot about Jesus as an adult. Listen to this verse that tells us about Jesus as a boy: "And the child grew and became strong; he was filled with wisdom, and the grace of God was upon him." We already talked about what it takes to grow physically and become strong.** Ask:

- **How do you learn?**
- **How do you learn more about God?**
- **How do you grow in wisdom?**

Say: **At school we learn things like reading, writing, and math.** Add ideas the kids mentioned. **We learn more about God by going to church, listening to Christian teachers, praying, and worshipping.**

Add ideas the kids mentioned. **Wisdom is what we *do* with the information we've learned. Let's make wise choices with all we learn. One wise thing we can do is tell people all we learn about Jesus! Let's ask God to help us grow like Jesus.**

Ask kids to crouch low and gradually get higher as you pray. **Dear God, thanks for Jesus who grew up just like us. Help us grow in all we know about you, so we can tell others about how much you love us.** Ask kids to stand and stretch tall as they say with you: **In Jesus' name, amen.**

Jesus Is Tempted (1)

Topic: Temptation

Scripture: Luke 4:1-13

Simple Supplies: You'll need a Bible, napkins, and cupcakes (or other treats) for the kids.

Gather the children, and give each of them a cupcake on a napkin. Say: **Don't eat your cupcake yet. I'll tell you the story about when Jesus was tempted in the wilderness. Listen to the story, but don't eat your cupcake until you hear the words "the end." OK?**

Show children your Bible open to Luke 4:1-13.

After Jesus was baptized, he was led by the Spirit to the desert, where for forty days he was tempted by the devil. Jesus didn't eat a thing for forty days! The devil told Jesus, "If you are the Son of God, tell this stone to become bread." Jesus told the devil, "Man does not live on bread alone." Ask the children to repeat the phrase.

Then the devil led Jesus to a high place. Ask the children to stand up. **The devil said that if Jesus would worship him, he'd give Jesus the world. But Jesus said, "No. I worship God only."** Ask the children to repeat the phrase.

Then the devil led Jesus to the highest point on the Temple. Ask the children to march in place, or get up on the step or stage. Or they could get on their tiptoes. **The devil told Jesus that if he was truly the Son of God to throw himself down, because the Bible said the angels would guard Jesus. Jesus said, "Don't put God to the test!"** Ask kids to repeat the phrase, then have them sit down. **Then the devil left Jesus.** *The end!* Let the children eat their cupcakes. Ask:

- **How did you feel as you waited to eat your scrumptious treat?**
- **How was it like Jesus being tempted in the desert?**
- **When we are tempted to do wrong things, who should we listen to?**

Say: **Jesus stood strong against the devil by knowing God's Word. Jesus is the Son of God, and Jesus knows God's Word. When we are tempted, we can pray to Jesus to help us be strong and to do what's right. Jesus is God's strong Son. Jesus is stronger than the devil who tempts us.**

Close by praying: **Jesus, I am so glad you were able to be strong against the devil when he tempted you. You know what it is like to be tempted. Please help us when we are tempted to do bad things. You are strong and powerful and you love me. Thank you! In your name, amen.**

Jesus Is Tempted (2)

Topic: Keep Focused

Scripture: Luke 4:1-13

Simple Supplies: You'll need a Bible, two chairs, one spoon, and one golf ball (or hardboiled egg). Place the chairs about fifteen feet apart.

Open your Bible to Luke 4:1-13, and say: **The Bible tells us that when Jesus was ready to start his work for God, Satan decided to tempt him and distract him from doing what God wanted him to do. That's the way Satan works, isn't it? He wants to distract us and make us forget what God wants us to do.**

Let's play a game called "Keep Focused." Do your parents ever tell you that? "When you do your homework, you better keep focused!" It means don't let anyone or anything keep you from doing what needs to get done.

First I need a volunteer to try to keep focused during our game. Choose someone, and give the volunteer the spoon with the golf ball on it. **Your job is to walk from this chair to the other one while holding your golf ball on the spoon. You must keep your eyes on the opposite chair at all times. Do not look away. Sound easy? But wait! The rest of you will be the "distracters."** Form two lines of kids along the path between the two chairs. **When I say, "Ready? Keep focused!" your job will be to try to get the volunteer to look away from the goal. Distraction techniques can be saying things like "Here, I'll carry it for you" or "Look over there!" You can't touch the volunteer. Ready? Keep focused!** Play the game several times, depending on how much time you have. Then ask:

- **Was it easy or hard for you to keep focused with the distractions? Why?**
- **How do you think it was for Jesus when Satan tried to distract him from his mission?**

Say: **Jesus was tempted by Satan to step aside from his mission. But Jesus kept his focus. Jesus knew what God wanted him to accomplish. When we are tempted to lose our focus from what God wants us to do, we can pray for God's help to stay focused. We can come to church and we can hang out with "focused" friends, too.**

Have the children sit in a row or two between the two chairs and pass the golf ball down the line as you close in prayer: **Dear God, I am so glad that you have a plan for me. Help me stay focused on what you want me to do and not be distracted by temptations. Thank you for Jesus who didn't lose his focus. In his name, amen.**

The Good Samaritan

Topic: Caring for Others

Scripture: Luke 10:25-37

Simple Supplies: You'll need a Bible, a baby doll, a red marker, enough bandages for each child and one for the doll, a crib or place to lay the doll down, and play money. Mark one of the doll's knees so it looks like an "owie."

Say: **This baby needs some tender loving care! She has a skinned knee, and we need to do something to make it feel better.** Ask:

- **What should we do to make the baby feel better?**
- **When you are hurt, what do people do to make you feel better?**

Say: **We could put a bandage on this doll's knee to make it feel better.** Put a bandage on its knee as you continue. **When we're hurt, our friends or family might hug us and put bandages on owies.** Mention other ideas the kids said.

Open your Bible to Luke 10:25-37, and show the kids the words. Say: **Our Bible story tells about a man who was hurt and who needed some care! Nobody stopped to help him! Two people came near but they walked right on by!**

Finally, one person did help. The person was from Samaria. Let's pretend this doll is the hurt man in the story. The good Samaritan bandaged the hurt man's wounds, like we did to our doll. Then he put the man on his donkey (lift up the doll) **and carried him to a place to rest** (place the doll in the crib). **Then he paid someone else to keep taking care of the hurt man because he couldn't stay.** Hold half of the money high.

He even said he'd come back when he was finished with his trip and pay more money (hold the other half of the money high) **if what he already gave wasn't enough. The amazing thing was that the good Samaritan didn't even know the hurt man, and he still went out of his way to care for him.** Ask:

- Why do you think Jesus wants us to be like the good Samaritan?
- Who can you show love and care to?

Say: **Jesus wants us to love and care for others, because Jesus loves everyone just the same. We can show love and care by being kind to our friends, by welcoming new people to our church, and by speaking nice words to our families, as well as helping sick and hurting people.**

Ask everyone to close their eyes and think of someone they can show care to this week. Give each child a bandage. Say: **Save this bandage to use to help someone.**

Then pray: **Dear God, help us be like the good Samaritan who went out of his way to show love and care. Help us do the same to people we meet. In Jesus' name, amen.**

Parable of the Lost Son

Topic: Forgiveness

Scripture: Luke 15:11-32

Simple Supplies: You'll need a Bible and an instrument for each child, such as noisemakers, tambourines, maracas, drums, or lids of pots and pans.

Open your Bible to Luke 15:11-32, and show the children the words. Say: **The Bible tells about a man who had two sons. One son asked for his share of the inheritance—which was money he was supposed to get when his dad died.**

The son gathered all he owned, went to a new country, spent all he had, and had a lot of big parties! Soon he ran out of money and was starving.

The son remembered that his dad's servants ate better than he was eating now. So he thought he'd go home, tell his dad he

was sorry, and ask if he could work for him. **Let's have one of you pretend you are the son who's coming home.** Choose a child to go to the opposite side of the room and stand. Hand out the instruments, and tell the kids not to play them yet, but do so when you say, "Let's celebrate!"

You know what happened? When the dad saw his son who was still a long way off, he was filled with love for him. The dad ran to his son! Run across the room to the child, and put your arm around him. **Then the dad said, "I love you son. Welcome home! Let's celebrate!"** Have the kids play the instruments while you lead the son to join the party. Ask:

- **When are we like the son?**
- **How is God like the father in the story?**

Say: **We might forget about God by not coming to church or not praying or when we do bad things. When we do, we should never be afraid to come back to God and say we're sorry. We can be like the son! God wants us with him so much he comes to meet us!**

Close by praying each line, then pausing after each for kids to repeat the line and play their instruments.

Dear God,
Thanks for Jesus!
Thanks for forgiving us!
Thanks for your great love!
In Jesus' name, amen.

Zacchaeus Sees Jesus

Topic: Jesus' Love

Scripture: Luke 19:1-10

Simple Supplies: You'll need a Bible, several adult volunteers, and a big poster or picture of Jesus.

Open your Bible to Luke 19, and show the children the words. Say: **The Bible tells about a man named Zacchaeus who very short. Everybody crouch down and pretend to be short Zacchaeus.** Ask:

- **What's it like down here?**
- **What can you see?**

Say: **It's hard to see things down here. If we were this short, we could get lost because we wouldn't see where we were going.**

In our story Zacchaeus might have been a bit frustrated. Jesus was coming into town, and there were so many people that he couldn't see over them. Have your adult volunteers come up and stand all around you in front of the kids so that the kids can no longer see you. Have kids stay in a crouched position, then ask them to jump up and down, trying to see over the taller adults.

Zacchaeus had an idea. He saw a tree and went over to it, and climbed way up to the top of the tree. Let's all pretend like we are climbing up the tree and we are getting taller and taller with every step. As kids are climbing taller and taller, have your adult volunteers couch down lower and lower, and bring out the poster of Jesus and hold it so everyone can see. Ask:

- **Now what do you see?**

Say: **We can all see Jesus! And do you know what? Jesus could see Zacchaeus. Jesus even told Zacchaeus to come down from the tree so that he could take Jesus to his house. Jesus wanted to be Zacchaeus' friend because he loved that little guy! Jesus loves us, too. He sees us all the time and wants to be our friend, no matter how short or little we may feel sometimes. Jesus loves us!**

Ask the kids to crouch low. Pray: **Dear God, thanks for loving Zacchaeus.** Ask kids to stretch tall, and hold up the picture of Jesus. **Thanks for loving us all the time, no matter how big or little we are. We love you, too. In Jesus' name, amen.**

Jesus Asks the Disciples to Remember Him

Topic: Remembering Jesus

Scripture: Luke 22:7-20

Simple Supplies: You'll need a Bible and five items to represent the five senses: sight, a picture of a party or celebration; touch, a soft blanket; hearing, party music; smell, a cinnamon-scented candle or air freshener; and taste, candy canes.

(ALLERGY ALERT)

Say: **When God made us, he gave us five senses.** Ask:

• **What are the five senses?**

Say: **The five senses are sight, touch, hearing, smell, and taste. These senses help us learn about and remember things.** Ask:

• **How does sight help us remember?**

Show the picture of a party or celebration. Say: **When we look at pictures, we remember fun parties and being with people we love.** Ask:

• **How about touch?**

Show and let children touch the soft blanket. Say: **This soft blanket could remind us of babies.** Ask:

• **What about hearing?**

Play an upbeat song. Say: **Listening to songs could remind us of Bible stories or of fun times we had learning the music.** Ask:

• **What about smell?**

Let kids smell the candle. Depending on the scent, cinnamon could remind them of their favorite dessert. Ask:

• **Finally, what about taste?**

Pass out the candy canes, and let kids eat them. Say: **Candy canes remind us of Christmas.**

While the children are eating their candy canes, open your Bible to Luke 22:7-20, and show the children the words. Say: **One of the most important things we can remember using our senses is how much God loves us. The Bible tells us about Jesus teaching his disciples. Jesus knew he was going away and he wanted his disciples to remember him. Jesus knew he would soon die, then rise again to be with God in heaven. Jesus gave the disciples bread and wine. They could see it, feel it, taste it, smell it, and even hear the bread crust break. Each time we share the bread and the wine, we remember Jesus.**

Close by praying: **Thank you, God, for our sense of smell, our sense of taste, our sense of sight, our sense of touch, and our sense of hearing.** Hold up each item as you talk about the senses. **Thank you for giving us such a wonderful way to remember what Jesus did for us with the bread and wine.**

 When asked "What do we call the special meal Jesus had with his disciples before he died?" nine-year-old Dane answered, "A potluck?"

Jesus Turns Water Into Wine (1)

Topic: Miracles

Scripture: John 2:1-11

Simple Supplies: You'll need a Bible, two clear pitchers, water, one package of red, pre-sweetened Kool-Aid mix, a spoon, enough small paper cups for each child, and a table.

Before the message, place the red Kool-Aid mix in the bottom of one pitcher. Fill the other pitcher with water, then set both pitchers on top of a table.

Open your Bible to John 2:1-11, and show the kids the words. Say: **Jesus attended a wedding once, and after a while they were out of wine. The guests had nothing left to drink, and the party was going to be ruined. So Jesus used his power to turn some large containers of water** (hold up the pitcher of clear water) **into wine.** Pour the water into the other pitcher. The water will turn red as it combines with the Kool-Aid mix. Hold it up high for all to see. Ask:

- **What did you think when you saw the water turn colors up here?**
- **What do you think the people thought when Jesus turned water into wine?**
- **What other miracles did Jesus do?**

Say: **What I showed you up here wasn't a real miracle. I had red Kool-Aid in a pitcher. When it mixed with water, it turned red. When Jesus turned water into wine, it was a true miracle. In fact, the people at the wedding were so amazed because the wine Jesus made tasted better than any other wine the host served.**

Jesus could do miracles because Jesus is God's Son—the creator of everything! Jesus did a lot of miracles when he lived on earth. He fed five thousand people, he healed people, and he raised people from the dead! Add others the kids mentioned. **Let's tell everyone about Jesus, who is God's Son and the creator of everything.**

LEADER

If you have a large number of children who will be coming up front, prepare several pitchers of Kool-Aid, and have volunteers ready to help you serve the drink.

Quickly stir the Kool-Aid in the pitcher, and give each child a very small amount in a cup. Ask the children to wait until you pray before drinking. Pray: **Jesus, your miracles show you are truly God. We want to let everyone know that you love him or her. Help us tell others. Thanks for coming to save us and show us your power! In your name, amen.**

Jesus Turns Water Into Wine (2)

Topic: Gifts

Scripture: John 2:1-11

Simple Supplies: You'll need a Bible, a table, and a flower bouquet that has been taken apart. During the message you'll put the bouquet together again, or you can ask a florist to do it.

As the children come forward, give each one a piece of the bouquet such as a flower, greenery, ribbon, or wrapping. Open your Bible to John 2:1-11, and say: **Once when Jesus, his disciples, and his mother went to a wedding, an embarrassing thing happened. The host of the wedding ran out of wine. Now that might not seem to be much to you. If you go to a party and your friend runs out of pizza or soda, you just run to the store and get some more. But in Jesus' time, there weren't many stores and when you ran out of food or drink for your guests, you'd be embarrassed. Besides, the party would be over.**

So when Jesus' mother asked him to help, he did it. He saw some containers for water, and he asked that they be brought to him. Jesus told some servants to fill the containers with water. And what do you think happened! Jesus turned water into wine! Wow! Jesus can do amazing things like that because he is Lord of all creation.

When we bring our gifts to Jesus, he can do amazing things as well. You all received something when you came up here. Hold them high so we can see. Pause while kids do this. **What nice gifts. Now let's see what happens when we bring our gifts together here at the table.** Invite the children forward, and arrange their gifts into a bouquet. If you have a florist, have him or her begin working. As you are working, say: **God gives such good gifts to his children. One flower by itself is pretty, but look what happens when our gifts are being used together.** Ask:

- **What gifts has Jesus given to you?** Kids might say, "I can sing," "I'm good at meeting new people," "I'm kind to my brother," and so on.

Keep the discussion going until the bouquet is completed. Hold it up high so everyone can see. Ask:

- **Isn't it beautiful?**
- **Do you see your item in there?**

Say: **In our church, we have many gifts to offer. When we bring them all to Jesus, he will do amazing things with them. Let's take this bouquet and place it in our church where everyone can see it. Then later, I'll give it away to someone who might need to be cheered up. Maybe some of you will be able to come along. Who knows? Maybe God gave you the gift of making people feel loved.**

Close with prayer: **Thank you, God, for the wonderful gifts you give. The best gift of all was Jesus. He does amazing things with what we bring to him, if it is empty wine jars, or talents and abilities. Help me use my gifts for you. Thanks for all you do for me! In Jesus' name, amen.**

Jesus Clears the Temple to Worship God

Topic: Honoring God

Scripture: John 2:13-16

Simple Supplies: You'll need a Bible and three pictures: a church, a farm, and a store.

LEADER TIP

Find pictures in magazines to show the kids. Or, if possible, use a digital camera for the pictures, then project them on a screen for the entire church to see.

Welcome the children, and show them the three photos of the church, the farm, and the store. Ask:

- **What is the building in each photo?**
- **What happens in each kind of building?**

Say: **We have a picture of a church, a farm, and a store. Each building is for something different.**

A church is for worshipping God. Add ideas kids said.

A farm is for raising animals and crops. Add ideas kids said.

And a store is for selling things and making money. Add ideas kids said. Ask:

- **What would happen if a farmer would try to work out of a church?**
- **What if a pastor would try to work out of a farm?**
- **What would happen if a store owner would try to work out of a church?**

Open your Bible to John 2:13-16. Say: **That's kind of what happened in our Bible story. Jesus went into Jerusalem and went to the Temple, which is like a church.** Ask:

- **What do you expect to happen in church?**

Say: **When Jesus got to the Temple, he thought he was at a farm or at a store! Jesus saw men selling cattle, sheep, and doves. Jesus saw others sitting at tables exchanging money. Jesus got very upset! That's not what you do in church! Church is for worshipping God!**

So Jesus drove everyone from the Temple area, even the sellers of sheep and cattle; he scattered the coins of the money-changers and overturned their tables. Jesus cleared the area! Ask:

- **What would you feel if you came to church and saw those things in our church?**
- **Why do you think Jesus was so mad?**

Say: **Jesus was upset that people were trying to sell things in God's house. The people had made it into a store. They made it into a farm with lots of animals! God's house is where the best thing of all, the gift of salvation, is totally free. The Temple and the church are for worshipping God.**

Lead the children in a prayer. Have them do what you say during the prayer. Pray: **Dear God, thank you for your church. Thank you for its foundation in your Word.** Have four kids lay in a square. **Thank you for its walls that surround your people.** Have some kids stand as walls. **Thank you for the high ceiling or steeple.** Have one or two kids create a steeple with upraised hands. **And thank you for your amazing Son, Jesus.** Have a child hold both arms out like a cross. **We are so glad that we worship in a church, where salvation is a free gift and costs us nothing. In Jesus' name, amen.**

Jesus and Nicodemus

Topic: Jesus Is the Light

Scripture: John 3:1-21

Simple Supplies: You'll need a Bible, a shoe box, a flashlight, construction paper, tape, and scissors. Tape a construction paper cross to the inside of one end of a shoe box. Cut a quarter-size hole opposite the cross. Cut a hole in the lid of the shoe box large enough to insert the end of a flashlight. Cover the top hole with dark construction paper.

Open your Bible to John 3, and say: **The Bible tells about a Jewish ruler named Nicodemus who came to Jesus at night to talk. Nicodemus had friends who didn't like Jesus, so Nicodemus didn't want them to see him meet with Jesus.**

When Jesus talked to Nicodemus, he said that the Light had come into a dark world. He was trying to get Nicodemus to understand that Jesus came to bring the truth about God to people who need him. We

need Jesus—who is the Light of the world—so we can live forever with him in heaven. Let's try an experiment, and I'll show you what Jesus meant.

Let the children take turns looking in the quarter-size hole inside the box. Ask them what they see. They'll probably say, "Nothing" or "It's too dark."

Next, take the paper off the top hole and shine a flashlight into the box. Then let the kids look through the quarter-size hole. Ask them what they see. They will be able to see the cross. Ask:

- **Do you think the cross was there the whole time? Why couldn't we see it before?**
- **What did we need to be able to see it?**

Say: **The cross was there the whole time. We needed light to see it. In the Bible, Jesus says that he is the light in the darkness. We need the light to have eternal life. We need Jesus! But so do other people. There are still lots of people who don't know the truth about Jesus. We can be Jesus' light to others, too, when we tell them about Jesus, when we bring them to church, and when we are kind with our words and actions.**

Shine the flashlight through the hole, and have all kids say with you: **Thank you, Jesus, for being light in the darkness. Amen.**

The Samaritan Woman

Topic: Living Water

Scripture: John 4:5-42

Simple Supplies: You'll need a Bible, and a straw and cup of water for each child.

Open your Bible to John 4:5-42, and show the children the words. Say: **One day, Jesus walked through a place called Samaria. While** he was there, he got thirsty. He came to a town and sat down by the town well, which is a big hole that contains water. A Samaritan woman came by, and Jesus asked, "Will you give me a drink?" Give each child a cup of water. Tell them not to drink it yet. **The woman thought it was very strange that Jesus asked her for a drink because in those days Samaritans and Jews didn't like each other, and men were supposed to stay separate from women.**

LEADER

If you can find one, bring a desktop water fountain and plug it in. There are also some tabletop water fountains that are battery powered. Do the message by the water fountain.

Jesus told the woman things about her life that only the woman knew about! She had made some bad decisions in her past. Jesus knew all about them!

Then Jesus told her that if she had asked *him* for water, he would give her living water. Give the kids each a straw, and have them blow into their cup of water so it bubbles.

Jesus was talking about his love being like living water. With Jesus' love in our hearts, it bubbles and bubbles, like when you are blowing into your water. You want to share Jesus' love with others! With Jesus' love in our hearts, we know we'll live forever with him. We want our friends and families and everyone to know, so we all can live with Jesus forever. Have kids blow into their water again.

When the woman figured out that Jesus had been sent by God, she was so excited she told lots and lots of people in her town. Ask:

• **Who is someone you can tell about Jesus?**

Say: **Let's tell everyone about Jesus and living with him forever.**

Pray: **Jesus, thank you so much for your love in our hearts that can be like living water. We are so glad we get to live with you forever. Help us tell others this good news! In your name, amen.**

Jesus Feeds 5,000

Topic: Miracles

Scripture: John 6:1-15

Simple Supplies: You'll need a Bible, five small loaves of bread, two cans of tuna, and twelve baskets (such as bread baskets or large bowls).

Say: **Hi everybody! I'm kind of hungry. I wonder if anyone else here is hungry.** Pause. **I wonder if everyone else in the church is hungry too. Hmm. I wonder how much food I'd need to feed everyone in this room and our entire church. Good thing I planned ahead and brought some food to feed all these hungry people here.**

Bring out the five small loaves of bread and two cans of tuna. Ask:

• **How many people do you think we could feed with five loaves of bread and two cans of tuna?**

Say: **We might be able to feed several people, but we wouldn't be able to feed our whole church.**

Open your Bible to John 6:1-15, and show the children the words. Say: **The Bible tells about Jesus who was with a crowd of five thousand people...and they were hungry! Five thousand people would be like all the people in this room, again, and again, and again...part of a city! Bigger than our church.** Fill in a description depending on the size of your church.

Jesus asked one of his disciples named Philip, "Where shall we buy bread for these people to eat?" Jesus asked this to test Philip, to see what he'd say. Philip said that if you worked eight months and used all your paychecks, it wouldn't be enough to feed that *huge* crowd.

Well, some other disciples brought a young boy to Jesus. The young boy had five loaves of bread (hold up a loaf) **and two fish.** Hold up a can of tuna. **Jesus had the huge crowd sit down. Then he took the boy's loaves, gave thanks, then gave the food to the crowd.**

You might think, "No way that crowd of five thousand people would get full on just a little bread (hold up a loaf) and a little bit of fish. Hold up a can of tuna. But when they had all had *enough* to eat—that means they were full—Jesus told the disciples to gather the leftovers.** One at a time, hand one of the twelve baskets to a child, and have

LEADER

If you have a small group of children, let each child hold a few baskets and hold them up one at a time as you count.

the children stand in a line. **The disciples filled twelve baskets with the leftovers!** Lead the kids in counting, "One," "two," "three," and so on, up to twelve. Have the kids who are holding the baskets lift them high as the rest of the kids count. Ask:

- **What do you think was amazing about this story?**
- **What amazing things does Jesus do today?**

Say: **I think it was amazing that so many people were fed with five loaves of bread and two fish. I also think it was amazing that Jesus used a little boy to work this miracle. There were lots of adults in that crowd of five thousand, but it was a little boy who stepped forward with his food to share. Jesus uses us to do amazing things today. We reach out to others to tell them about Jesus, we help those in need, and we encourage each other as we grow in our faith.**

Ask seven kids to hold the five loaves of bread and two cans of tuna. Pray: **Dear Jesus, thanks for using a little boy to make a great miracle. Thanks for using his five loaves of bread and two fish to feed five thousand people. Please use us to do good for you today and always. We love you so. In Jesus' name, amen.**

Jesus Washes the Disciples' Feet

Topic: Service

Scripture: John 13:1-17

Simple Supplies: You'll need a Bible, a towel, a basin of water, and wet wipes.

Open your Bible to John 13, and show the kids the words. Say: **Jesus used a bowl of water** (raise it high) **and a towel** (raise it high)**, and he washed his disciples' feet. In Jesus' day, people wore sandals and would walk along dirt roads. When they'd reach a place, the lowest of the servants would wash their feet. Well,** *Jesus* **washed the disciples' feet. Jesus is God's Son! But he wanted his disciples to know that we need to serve others.** Ask:

- **How did Jesus serve others when he lived on earth?**
- **How can we serve each other?**
- **Why do you think Jesus wants us to serve others?**

Say: **Not only did Jesus wash his disciples' feet, he served us more than anyone has ever done. He gave us life so that we could live with him forever. Jesus loves us so much that he did that for us!**

We can serve each other in so many ways. We can help with chores around the house, we can help a neighbor carry in groceries, we can look out for new kids and make them feel welcome, we can bring our friends to church to learn about Jesus. Jesus wants us to serve others so they see Jesus in us.

Close by praying: **Dear Jesus, you gave us a wonderful example of how you want us to serve others. Help us see the ways you want us to help others and show them your love.**

Give each child a wet wipe. Say: **As you go back to your seat, take one of these wipes, and wipe off the hands of your parents or a family member. Tell them one thing you can do to serve them this week, even if it's the dirty work like cleaning the** bathrooms! Then hang up the wipe somewhere in your house where you will see it, and let it remind you to do the thing you said that you'd do.

God Sends His Holy Spirit

Topic: The Holy Spirit

Scripture: Acts 2:1-21; 3:12-19

Simple Supplies: You'll need a Bible, a portable radio (turned on and tuned to a Christian radio station) with a cord and with the batteries removed, and a flashlight. Position yourself near an outlet.

Bring out the radio, but don't plug it in yet. Ask:

- **Who knows how we get a radio to work?**

Say: **Invisible electricity gets a radio to work. We get it from a cord or batteries.** Show kids how the radio doesn't work yet because it's not plugged in and there are no batteries. **Let's use this radio to learn about our Bible story today.** Open your Bible to Acts 2:1-21, and show the children the words.

After Jesus died and then rose again, all of the people who believed in him were gathered in one place. All of a sudden they heard a sound like the blowing of a strong wind. Ask everyone to sound like the wind. **Then the believers saw what looked like a flame of fire above the heads of each one of them.** Shine the flashlight on each child's head, then over to the radio. Ask a child to hold the flashlight for you so you can plug in the cord. **The fire was a sign of the Holy Spirit.**

The Holy Spirit gave the believers power to do great things. Plug in the radio so music comes out loudly, and then turn down the volume. **One of the things the Holy Spirit gave the believers was**

power to speak different languages so that everyone all over the world could learn about Jesus' life, death, and resurrection! Ask:

- Why did God give the Holy Spirit to the believers?
- Why does God give us the Holy Spirit?
- Who can we tell about Jesus?

Say: **One reason God gave the Holy Spirit to the believers was so they could speak new languages and go all around the world** telling people about Jesus. God gives us the Holy Spirit to help us live like Jesus and to tell others about him.

LEADER

When using a flashlight to shine on the children, be very careful to keep the light away from the children's eyes.

Keep the music playing softly as you shine the flashlight on each child. Pray: **Dear God, thank you for the Holy Spirit's power that helps us tell everyone about you. In Jesus' name, amen.**

An Angel Frees Peter From Jail

Topic: Helping Others

Scripture: Acts 12:1-18

Simple Supplies: You'll need a Bible and a flashlight. Set the flashlight close by, yet where kids can't see it.

Open your Bible to Acts 12:1-18, and show the children the words. Say: **Our Bible story is about Peter, who was in jail. Peter was one of Jesus' special friends called an** *apostle* **who told everyone about Jesus' life, death, and resurrection. The rulers of the day didn't want people to talk about Jesus. So they caught Peter and threw him in jail. They chained Peter's wrists together so he couldn't escape.** Have everyone grasp his or her own wrists tightly.

Then they had some guards stand by Peter so he really couldn't escape. All the while Peter was in jail, his friends who also believed in Jesus were praying for him.

Peter fell asleep, and when he woke up, he had a big surprise. **Everyone close your eyes, don't peek, and pretend to sleep. Keep holding your wrists.** While kids are "sleeping" and "snoring," turn on the flashlight. Go to the kids and say: **Quick! Get up! Quick! Get up! An angel—that's me if you have a very good imagination—woke up Peter, and light filled the jail. The angel made the chains fall off of Peter's wrists, so let go of your own wrists. Then the angel led him past the guards and to a safe spot. The guards didn't even notice Peter was gone until the next morning! Peter's friends were extremely surprised to see Peter. They were so thankful to God that their prayers had been answered.** Ask:

- How do you think Peter felt when he woke up?
- How did you feel when I "woke you up"?
- How did the angel help Peter?
- How did his friends help Peter?

Say: **I think Peter was surprised when he woke up and saw an angel. For a while he thought he was dreaming or seeing a vision. But Peter knew it was real when the angel helped him escape and led him to a safe place. Peter's friends helped Peter by praying for him. God answered the prayers.**

Ask the children to think of someone who needs help. Maybe someone who is sick, maybe someone who is poor, or maybe someone who just lost a spouse. Lead kids in praying for the person in need, just like the friends prayed for Peter when he needed help getting out of jail. Pray: **Dear God, thank you for the example of how Peter's friends prayed for him. Please help...**(pause for children to silently pray). **We know you don't always send an angel to solve problems, but you are always there helping us. We love you. In Jesus' name, amen.**

Lydia Is Converted

Topic: Family of God

Scripture: Acts 16:9-15

Simple Supplies: You'll need a Bible, several pictures of people from magazines, and a purple cloth.

Unfurl the purple cloth, and say: **Our Bible story today is about a woman named Lydia who was a "dealer in purple cloth." She could have been a businessperson who made the cloth or sold it. Before I tell you more about our Bible story, which is found in Acts 16:9-15 in our Bibles, I have a few questions to ask you.**

One at a time, hold up a picture, and ask:

• **Does God want this person to be a part of the family of God?**

When kids respond "yes," ask one person to stand up front and hold the picture. Do this for several pictures so you have several kids standing up front. Then ask a girl to drape the purple cloth over her shoulders to represent Lydia.

Say: **God wants everyone to be a part of the family of God.**

Show children your Bible, open to Acts 16:9-15.

Say: **Lydia was a dealer in purple cloth. She heard Paul tell about Jesus, and then she believed in Jesus. In fact, Lydia and her whole household were baptized. Then she invited Paul to come to her home and eat!** Ask:

• **Do you think God wanted Lydia to be a part of the family of God?**

Kids will say "yes," so have "Lydia" join the crowd up front.

Say: **God wants all of us to be a part of his family!** Ask all of the children to cluster together like one big, happy family. Then close in prayer: **God, I am so very glad that you want everyone to become a part of your family. Help me to tell others that they can become part of your family. In Jesus' name, amen.**

Paul and Silas Go to Jail

Topic: Courage

Scripture: Acts 16:16-34

Simple Supplies: You'll need a Bible.

Ask:

- **Who likes to sing?**
- **When do you sing?**

Say: **Some people love to sing! They sing in their cars, in the shower, at church, and lots of places.** Add places the kids mentioned too. Open your Bible to Acts 16:16-34, and show the children the words.

The story of Paul and Silas teaches us that even when we're scared, we can sing and praise God. Paul and Silas were telling people about Jesus' life, death, and resurrection. The rulers of the day didn't want others to hear about Jesus. So they had Paul and Silas beaten, thrown in prison, and chained so they couldn't escape. That seems pretty bad to me. But no matter how bad their situation, Paul and Silas knew that God loved them and whatever happened God would be with them. Even when their lives looked sad, they still remembered that God loved them, and that made them extremely happy. So they sang. Ask:

- **When have you been scared?**

Say: **When you're scared, be like Paul and Silas. Remember that God loves you and he is with you, and sing a song. Let's do it now.** Name a scary situation the children mentioned, such as "being in a thunderstorm." Then lead kids in singing "Jesus Loves Me." Name at least three scary situations, and sing "Jesus Loves Me" after each one.

**Jesus loves me! This I know, for the Bible tells me so;
Little ones to him belong, they are weak but he is strong.**

LEADER TIP

Sing a simple well-known song such as "Jesus Loves Me" for this message. You could ask a pianist to accompany you as well, or play a children's version on your sound system.

Yes, Jesus loves me! Yes, Jesus loves me!
Yes, Jesus loves me! The Bible tells me so.

Say: **Other people in jail with Paul and Silas heard them praying and singing. All of a sudden there was a violent earthquake.** Have the kids move around like the ground is shaking.

The jail doors flew open, and all the prisoners' chains came loose. The guard thought the prisoners would escape and that he'd get in big trouble. He was going to kill himself, but Paul shouted, "Don't harm yourself, we are all here!"

The guard had heard Paul and Silas praising God and wanted to know how to be saved. Paul and Silas told him about Jesus. The guard took the prisoners to his home, washed their wounds, fed them a meal, and he and his whole family were baptized!

Close in prayer: **Dear God, thanks for the example of Paul and Silas. There are times when we are scared, but help us remember that you still love us and that you will always be with us.**

Lead the children in singing "Jesus Loves Me" one more time.

 After the children's message, the leader asked five-year-old Turner what he thought about the lesson. "It was OK. But all the talk about God gives me a headache."

Messages for Topical Stories

Instructions for Life

Topic: The Bible

Scripture: Deuteronomy 11:18

Simple Supplies: You'll need a Bible, a loaf of bread, tub of butter, jar or squeeze container of jelly, two butter knives, paper plates, and napkins. Set the supplies on top of a table.

Say: **I'm so excited to see all of you today, so I brought stuff to make a snack to share.** Hold up the ingredients as you list them. **I've got the butter, the jelly, the bread, the knives, and even some plates and napkins. So let's put this whole thing together!** Pause, scratching head—as if thinking a minute. **Hmmm...I've got all these great ingredients here, but there are so many ways to make the snack...I need instructions!**

Make several attempts to make the sandwich, humorously, such as placing a slice of bread on the table, then stacking the jars on top of it. Ask the children to guide you through the process, making sure to do literally every step they tell you. For example, if they say "Put butter on the bread," place the tub of butter on a slice of bread. Finally, make a sandwich the right way. Say: **Wow, that was confusing! It sure would have been helpful if I'd remembered exactly how to make that snack or if I'd had some instructions!**

Ask another adult to make sandwiches for all of the children while you discuss:

- **What do we need instructions for in life?**
- **What happens if you don't follow instructions?**

Say: **We need instructions for fixing food, for driving cars, for walking across streets, and for putting together toys or furniture.** Add other ideas kids mentioned. **The best instructions we need in life are right here.** Hold up the Bible.

God gave us the Bible so we don't have to guess and make wrong choices, like I did when I was first making our snack. Let's see what the Bible tells us about God's Word. Open the Bible to Deuteronomy 11:18, and read: **"Fix these words of mine in**

your hearts and minds; tie them as symbols on your hands and bind them on your foreheads." When we read the Bible and listen to others tell us about Jesus, we know how to live each day. We don't have to guess. It's all right here! Hold up the Bible one more time.

Pass out sandwiches to everyone, and say: **Thanks for giving me instructions on how to make our snack. Remember to follow God's instructions in the Bible.** Close with prayer: **Thank you, God, that you love us so much that you gave us the Bible. Help us always remember your Word, the Bible, has our instructions for life. Amen.**

Word Power

Topic: Affirmation

Scripture: Proverbs 16:24

Simple Supplies: You'll need a Bible, a jar of honey, a bag of large pretzel sticks, and napkins.

Say: **Hi, everyone! You all look** *maaahh-velous* **today! You all have such bright, smiley faces that always make me smile too.**

Take a few seconds to say something nice to someone sitting by you. Pause while kids do this. **We feel good when people tell us kind things, right?**

I was wondering who can complete this sentence: Sticks and stones may break my bones, but...(words will never hurt me). Ask:

• **Is that true, that words will never hurt you? Why or why not?**

Say: **Words can hurt us!** Hold up a bag of pretzel sticks so everyone can see. Then give a pretzel to each child. **Let's pretend that these pretzels are our bones—let's say an arm. Now when someone says something kind to us, like we just said to one another, that's** like getting a pat on the shoulder, or on the arm. Turn to people next to you and pat their shoulders. Pause.

Great! When someone says bad words to us like "You're stupid" or "I don't like you," those words really hurt. It's like instead of patting us on our arm, they break our bone! Everyone break your pretzel "bone" in the middle. Pause. *Ouch!* Let's see what the Bible tells us about our words. Open your Bible to Proverbs 16:24, and read: **"Pleasant words are a honeycomb, sweet to the soul and healing to the bones."**

Take out the jar of honey. Give each person a napkin. Say: **Let's practice using nice, sweet-tasting words. Each of you can have a chance. When you say nice words, like "I love you" or "You are my friend," dip your pretzel in the honey. The Bible says pleasant words are healing to the bones!**

After the children do this, say: **Let's make sure our words are always sweet like honey.**

Close in prayer: **Dear God, help us to remember how powerful our words are, to heal or to harm. We need your help to use our words to do good and to tell others about you.**

Let each person tell God an affirming "We love you, amen!"

An Explosion!

Topic: Anger

Scripture: Ephesians 4:26

Simple Supplies: You'll need a Bible and a two-liter bottle of pop.

Hold the container of pop, and say: **Did you know that it's OK to feel angry? It's what we *do* with our anger that makes the difference.** Ask:

- **What are some things that make you angry?**

Repeat each response, and shake the container. After you get lots of responses, say: **OK, now I'll just open this container.** Wait for kids to respond "Nooooooooooooo! It'll explode!" **Oh! A lot of things can make us angry, but it's what we *do* with our anger that makes a difference!**

Let's see what the Bible says to do with our anger. Open your Bible to Ephesians 4:26, and read: **"In your anger do not sin: Do not let the sun go down while you are still angry."** That means, when we get angry we have to talk about it, or listen to quiet music, or go for a walk, or something so it doesn't make us explode (hold up the container) **and do something we'll be sorry for!** Ask:

- **Next time you get angry, what can you do so you don't explode?**

Close in prayer: **Dear God, we need your help when we are angry. Help us learn good things to do with our anger, and not to do things that are harmful. Thank you that you have given us the Bible that is so full of wisdom. In Jesus' name, amen.**

Who's the Boss?

Topic: Authority

Scripture: Matthew 28:18-20

Simple Supplies: You'll need a Bible and an inflated world globe ball.

Say: **We're going to talk a bit about who's the boss in our lives. But right now, I'm going to be the boss and tell you what to do. You have to do what I ask you to! I'll ask a question and then toss the globe ball to someone. Whoever catches it will answer the question then toss it back to me so I can ask another question. Do what I tell you because I'm the boss!**

LEADER

If you don't have a world globe ball, use a regular globe. Instead of catching the ball, kids could spin the globe.

- Who's the boss at your school?
- Who's the boss in your house?
- Who's the boss on a soccer team?
- Who's the boss at church?

Get the ball back, then open your Bible to Matthew 28:18-20. Say: **There are all kinds of "bosses" or authority figures in our lives. The Bible tells us that Jesus said: "All authority in heaven and on earth has been given to me. Therefore go and make disciples of all nations, baptizing them in the name of the Father and of the Son and of the Holy Spirit, and teaching them to obey everything I have commanded you. And surely I am with you always, to the very end of the age." Jesus is the boss of heaven and earth. He tells us to teach others about him. He's the boss, so let's obey!** Ask:

- **What's one way you can obey Jesus this week?**

Close by praying to our highest authority—Jesus: **Dear Jesus, we understand that you are our highest authority. Help us to be brave as we try to obey your command to teach others about you. You did so much for us and we love you. In your name we pray, amen.**

Hats Off to God

Topic: Loving God

Scripture: Deuteronomy 6:5

Simple Supplies: You'll need a Bible, a plastic foam bowl for each child, and a variety of hats (such as a fireman, construction worker, restaurant chef, baseball, and so on).

One at a time, hold up a hat and ask the children these questions:

- **What kind of a job do you think a person wearing this hat does?**
- **What would the person do at work?**

Say: **Those were great job descriptions! Did you know each of you has an important job too? In fact, it's the biggest job any of you will ever have in your entire life! You have the important job of following Jesus—being a Christian! There are many parts to our jobs as Christians, but all of them lead to one thing: showing God that we love him. Loving God is the most important part of our job as Christians.**

LEADER

If you have time in your children's message, have kids decorate their hats. Otherwise, have them decorate the hats at home. You could add a rim around the hats by gluing each one to a plate, letting the glue dry, then cutting a hole out of the plate so it leaves a rim.

Open the Bible to Deuteronomy 6:5, and read: **"Love the Lord your God with all your heart and with all your soul and with all your strength." Let's have some hats to remind us of the most important part of our job as Christians—loving God!**

Hand each person a bowl to wear as a hat. After you say each line of this prayer, have kids lift off their hats and say "We love you, God," then put them back on.

Dear God, thanks for giving us Jesus. We love you, God!
Thanks for helping us tell others about you. We love you, God!
Thanks for forgiving us. We love you, God.
Help us to always forgive others. We love you, God.
Thanks for letting us live forever with you. We love you, God.
We love being Christians! We love you, God.
In Jesus' name, amen. We love you, God.

Get Ready!

Topic: Sharing Faith

Scripture: Luke 3:7-18

Simple Supplies: You'll need a Bible and three groups of supplies: school supplies—such as a dictionary and lunch box; sports supplies—such as a soccer ball and shin guards; and winter wear supplies—such as a coat, hat, and gloves. Place the supplies in a jumbled pile on top of a table.

Say: **I have some things here that we use to get ready for important times. Let's see if we can figure out what they get us ready for. When I mention an important time, take turns gathering the things that would help us get ready. Put them in separate piles on the floor.** Ask:

- **If we knew winter was coming and it was going to get colder, what would we use to get ready?** Have kids gather the coat, hat, and gloves and place them in a pile. **What other things would we use?**
- **If we knew school was about to start, what would we use to get ready?** Have kids gather the school supplies in a pile. **What other things would we use?**
- **If we knew we had a soccer game coming up, what would we use to get ready?** Let volunteers form a pile of the soccer equipment. **What other things would we use?**

Open your Bible to Luke 3:7-18, and show the children the words. Say: **The Bible tells us about John the Baptist who helped people get ready for Jesus' coming. John told people to be kind and fair to one another. He said to love each other like God loved them. John the Baptist helped people prepare for God's chosen one!** Ask:

- **If you knew Jesus was coming to visit your house, what would you use to get ready?** Pause while kids respond.

Say: **If Jesus were coming to visit my house, I'd clean it really well, I'd make a good meal, I'd wear my best clothes, and I'd want to give him lots of presents!**

Let's be like John the Baptist and help people get ready for Jesus.
Tell the children of the upcoming activities your church has planned.
Encourage them to invite friends to come learn about Jesus! Close
with prayer: **Dear God, we want everyone to know about Jesus
and how wonderful he is. Please give us courage to be like John
the Baptist to help people get ready to meet Jesus. Amen.**

Hear! Hear!

Topic: God's Word

Scripture: Luke 2:39-52

Simple Supplies: You'll need a Bible.

Say: **We don't know a lot about Jesus when he was a child like
you. There is only one story about Jesus as a child.** Open your
Bible to Luke 2:39-52, and show the children the words. **When Jesus
was twelve years old, his parents, Mary and Joseph, took him to
the Temple in Jerusalem. The Temple was like a church, only
very, very big. When Jesus was at the Temple, he was listening
to the teachers and asking them questions. Jesus became so
interested in what his teachers were saying that when Mary and
Joseph left, he forgot to go with them! He stayed and listened,
and it took a while for his parents to come back and find him.**

**Listening to God's Word and to our teachers is how we grow
closer to God and how we grow strong in our faith. But listening
can be hard sometimes. Let's play a listening game. I'll read
about Jesus in the Temple, but every so often I'll include one of
your names. When you hear your name, raise your hand, then
put it back down.**

LEADER

Depending on the size of your group, insert two or three children's names each time you pause. If there are adults and teenagers listening in on the children's message, insert one of their names as well.

"After the Feast was over, while his parents were returning home [say a name], the boy Jesus stayed behind in Jerusalem, but they were unaware of it [say a name]. Thinking he was in their company, they traveled on for a day [say a name]. Then they began looking for him among their relatives and friends [say a name]. When they did not find him [say a name], they went back to Jerusalem to look for him. After three days they found him in the temple courts, sitting among the teachers [say a name], listening to them and asking them questions." Ask:

- Was it easy or hard for you to listen for your name as I read? Why?
- How do we listen to God's Word? Why is it important?

Say: **God wants you to listen to the Bible as though it were written especially for you. When we listen well to it, we will grow strong and wise, like Jesus did.**

Close in a prayer. **Dear God, please help all of us listen to your Word. In Jesus' name, amen.** Pass the Bible around the group, and say each child's name as he or she holds the Bible.

Afraid of Your Shadow

Topic: Facing Fears

Scripture: Isaiah 41:10

Simple Supplies: You'll need a Bible, an overhead projector, and a screen (or a blank wall).

Gather the children around you, and turn on the overhead projector.

Say: **Let's talk about things that make us afraid. I'll use my hands to make some shadow puppets. Tell me what you think each one is!** Make a shadow puppet of a dog with your hands between the lamp and the lens of the overhead projector so it casts a giant picture on the screen. Ask:

- **What do you think this is?** Pause.
- **Who is afraid of big dogs?**

Say: **I am!**

Form an "O" with each hand and place them together to look like eyes. Place this on the overhead projector and let kids guess. Say: **When I was little, I'd be afraid to look under my bed. I thought I would see eyes looking at me!**

Let several children take turns using their hands to make things they're afraid of. A simple one is to just form a "claw" with one hand and have it be a wild animal. Ask the other children to look at the screen and guess what the shadows are. Ask:

- **What do you do when you're afraid?**
- **What do you think God wants us to do when we're afraid?**

Open your Bible to Isaiah 41:10, and say: **This is what God tells us to do about fear: "So do not fear, for I am with you; do not be dismayed, for I am your God. I will strengthen you and help you; I will uphold you with my righteous right hand." God doesn't want us to be afraid. He tells us not to worry ourselves by looking at the things around us that make us afraid. God wants us to focus on him and trust that he holds us and supports us.**

Place a closed hand on the overhead projector. Ask the children to name five things they're afraid of. Open one finger each time they name something. After each one, have kids pray: "We give you our fears, God." After kids have named five things, your fingers will be open wide. Say: **You've given God your fears, now remember our verse that says not to fear because God will hold us in his hands.**

A seven-year-old named Tami asked, "How do we know the Bible is the Word of God?" Her five-year-old brother answered, "Because the words are in red."

Bending the Truth

Topic: Honesty

Scripture: Ephesians 4:25

Simple Supplies: You'll need a Bible, a metal coat hanger (preferably a colorful one with a rubber coating over the wire), two small foam balls, and a pair of trousers.

Hold up the coat hanger for everyone to see. Say: **Let's talk about honesty. Honesty is kind of like this coat hanger. Many important things hang on our honesty.** As you hold the hanger, have a child place the trousers on it. **People look at how honest you and I are before they decide whether to hang their trust on us.**

Sometimes, we can be tempted not to tell the truth. As you talk, take the trousers off the hanger, unwrap the two wire ends of the coat hanger from each other, and place a small foam ball over each end of the wire. **We might be afraid of getting in trouble with our mom or dad. We might be afraid that people won't like us unless we make up something exciting about ourselves.**

Let's pretend that you got a very bad grade on a test because you didn't want to study. Your parent asks you why you did so poorly on the test. I'll pass this wire around the group. When it gets to you, make up an excuse that you've heard people use to get out of trouble. After you say your excuse, bend the wire once and then pass it to the next person.

Excuses could be "I was too tired," "I was feeling sick," and "The teacher doesn't like me." Let the children take turns passing the coat hanger around and making up excuses. After everyone has had a turn, remove the foam balls from the wire and attempt to reconnect the ends.

Say: **Yuck! Look at this hanger. It doesn't look anything like it did when we started.** Ask:

- **Who would like to use a hanger like this? Why or why not?**
- **How is this hanger like what happens to us when we "bend the truth"?**

Open your Bible to Ephesians 4:25, and read it to the children: **"Therefore each of you must put off falsehood and speak truthfully to his neighbor, for we are all members of one body." God wants us to be able to trust each other so we can be close friends with each other. God knows that lying hurts friendships, even when we think we are just "bending" the truth a little bit. God wants us to be honest so people can hang their trust on our word.**

Pass the hanger from person to person, and let each pray: "Help us always tell the truth, Lord."

Lead the children in praying: **In Jesus' name, amen.**

Egg-citing Service

Topic: Service

Scripture: Exodus 18

Simple Supplies: You'll need a Bible, two cartons of one dozen eggs, two 6x15-inch pieces of plywood, a razor knife, and a tarp. Remove the lids of the egg cartons with the razor knife.

Lay the tarp on the ground (just in case). Set the two cartons of eggs on the ground parallel to each other with about six inches between them. Remove one egg from a carton and hold it up. Ask:

- **What would happen if I tried to place all my weight on this one egg?**

Say: **One egg all by itself can't hold a lot of weight. The shell is fragile and cracks when it's given a job to do that is too big for it.** Ask:

- **Have you ever had a job that was too big for you to handle? Did you ask for help?**

- **Can you think of any jobs that need to be done in the church that are too big for one person to do alone?**

Open your Bible to Exodus 18, and say: **God gave Moses the job of ruling the people of Israel. But it was too big of a job for Moses to do by himself. Moses wanted to serve God, but he was wearing himself out.**

Moses' father-in-law, Jethro, had a suggestion that helped Moses be the leader God wanted Moses to be. Jethro told Moses to get some help. His father-in-law, Jethro, told Moses to get help. Pick up the egg carton, and return the egg to its place. **Moses decided to get many other people to work with him. They all served God together, as a team.**

Look at these eggs. One egg alone couldn't support the weight of a person. Let's see if these twenty-four eggs can work together to hold someone up. Gently place one piece of plywood over each carton of eggs. Select a younger, light child to place a foot gingerly on each piece of plywood. Have other children stand on either side of the eggs to help the child onto the plywood. The eggs will support the child's weight. Ask:

- **Why do you think the eggs were able to hold up a whole person?**
- **How is this like what happens when we choose to serve God together?**

Say: **God wants us to serve him. God wants us to do some amazingly big jobs—jobs that we can't do on our own. However, when we serve together, we can do things that we never thought possible.**

Guide the children in choosing one way to serve God together. They could combine their offering to support a child from Compassion International or World Vision. Or they could work together to clean an elderly church member's house. Close with prayer: **Dear God, help these children understand that you want all of us to work together to do big things for you. Give us all the strength to do that and the wisdom to know what it is that you want us to do. In Jesus' name, amen.**

Time Saves

Topic: Jesus' Return

Scripture: 2 Peter 3:9

Simple Supplies: You'll need a Bible, two clean garbage cans, and enough inflated balloons to fill one of the garbage cans.

Gather the children by the two garbage cans, which are about five feet apart. Say: **After Jesus went to heaven, some of the people who believed in Jesus wanted him to come back right away. They wondered why Jesus took so long to come back to earth like he promised.**

So one of Jesus' friends named Peter wrote these words. Open your Bible to 2 Peter 3:9, and read: **"The Lord is not slow in keeping his promise, as some understand slowness. He is patient with you, not wanting anyone to perish, but everyone to come to repentance."**

Let's play a game that will help us understand why Jesus is patient and hasn't come back to earth yet. Let's pretend that the balloons in this garbage can are your most favorite toys ever. You love them and want to keep them forever. But then you learn that the garbage can they're in will be taken to the dump and destroyed! You have thirty seconds to save as many of your "toys" as you can by moving them from one garbage can to the other. Ready? Go!

Give the children thirty seconds to move the balloons. Call time, and ask:

- **Why weren't you able to save all of your toys?**
- **How did you feel trying to save all your toys in such a short amount of time?**

Say: **I'll be patient with you and give you a few more minutes to work.** Give kids three minutes, and let them finish "saving" the balloons. **It was frustrating not to be able to save all of your favorite toys. You know, God loves people far more than we love our favorite things. And God wants all people to live with him forever. So God is patient. He gives us time to tell our friends about Jesus. Even though it might seem that God is being slow in keeping his promise to come back, he's just being patient.**

Ask the children to close their eyes and picture one person they can tell about Jesus. Close with prayer: **Dear God, help us to tell people about Jesus. Thank you for being so patient and giving us time to tell lots of people. In Jesus' name, amen.**

Whaddya Know?

Topic: School

Scripture: Luke 2:46-52

Simple Supplies: You'll need a Bible.

Say: **School is such an important place, because you learn so many things you'll need to grow up to be happy adults.** Ask:

- **If you go to school, what are some of the favorite things you've learned so far?**
- **If you aren't in school yet, what's a favorite thing your parents or grandparents have taught you?**

Some of the answers could be "I learned how to sew a quilt," "I learned about how the early settlers traveled and ate," and so on.

Say: **What cool things you've learned! Did you know that Jesus was a learner too? When Jesus was a boy, he went to the Temple to learn. He sat with the people who taught God's Word.** Open your Bible to Luke 2:46, and say: **The Bible says that Jesus listened to the teachers and asked them questions.**

Let's do a simple activity. In a minute, I'll have you get with a partner and try to teach your partner the favorite thing you've learned. Help all the children find a partner. **When I say "go," both of you will try to teach your favorite thing to your partner. But you must talk at the same time. Ready? Go!** Give the children a minute to try to teach their partners. Ask:

- **How did you feel when you tried to teach someone who wasn't listening?**
- **Why is listening an important part of learning at school?**
- **How does asking questions help us learn at school?**

Say: **The Bible says that when Jesus was a boy, he learned many things. Jesus grew up physically. He also grew up in wisdom and in his relationship with God and everyone around him. It's important that you do your best in school so you can grow up in knowledge and wisdom, just like Jesus.**

Close in prayer: **Dear God, help these children to be good listeners so they can be good learners. I'm so glad they have you to help them in church, at school, and at home—anywhere they can learn. In Jesus' name, amen.**

Letting Go

Topics: Anger, Forgiveness

Scripture: Ephesians 4:26

Simple Supplies: You'll need a Bible and a bucket of medium-sized rocks (one rock for each child).

Give each of the children a rock to hold. Say: **Think for a moment about a time someone did something wrong to you. Maybe someone said something mean to you. Maybe a friend told a lie about you.** Pause. **When someone does something wrong to us, we have a choice. We can hold onto our anger and be mad at the person who hurt us, or we can let our anger go and forgive the person.**

Let's see what happens when we hold onto our anger. Everyone stand up and hold onto your rock. We are going to sing a song and do the motions. But you have to hold onto the rock the whole time.

Lead the children in singing and doing the motions to a song such as "Jesus Loves Me" or another familiar one. Encourage the children to hold onto their rocks the whole time. Ask:

- **What was it like doing the motions with the rock in your hand?**
- **How is this like what happens when we hold onto our anger?**

Open your Bible to Ephesians 4:26, and say: **God tells us that we can be angry but not to sin. And we are not to let the sun go down on our anger. That means don't hang onto our anger!** Ask:

- **How can we forgive others when they hurt us?**
- **How can we ask for forgiveness when we hurt others?**

Say: **We can pray to God and ask him to help us forgive others. We can ask others to forgive us when we hurt them. God loves us and doesn't want us to be miserable from carrying around our anger. When we let go of our anger, God helps us feel better.**

Ask the children to each place his or her rock back in the bucket and silently ask God's help in forgiving the person who's hurt him or her. Then sing the song again with free hands.

End with prayer: **Dear God, help us remember how hard it was to carry a rock and still praise you. Help us forgive others when they hurt us so we don't have to carry around our anger.**

 When asked to give examples of sin, one little boy raised his hand. When called on, he didn't say a word. He simply slapped the boy next to him on the back of the head.

Many Ways to Love

Topic: Love Each Other

Scripture: Galatians 5:13b-14

Simple Supplies: You'll need a Bible, work gloves, a greeting card, and a board game.

Give one child the work gloves, another child the greeting card, another child the board game. Ask them to stand up front with their items and spread out. Ask two other kids to stand up front by them, not holding anything.

Say: **There are so many ways we can show love to people.** Ask the child to hold up the work gloves. **These work gloves remind us that we can show love to people by being helpful and serving them.** Ask:

- **How can we serve others to show love?**

Say: **We can serve others by helping neighbors shovel their walks when it snows, or we can help a parent or guardian clean the house. When we serve others, we show love.**

Ask the child to hold up the greeting card. Say: **Another way we can show love to others is by telling them how important they are to us and how much we love them. We can send them cards or we can call them on the phone.** Ask:

- **What are some loving words we can share with people?**

Let the children say loving words to those close by, such as "You have a nice smile" or "Glad you're here today." Say: **When we send cards or say nice things, we show love to people.**

Ask the child to hold up the board game. **Another way we can let others know that we love them is to spend time with them. You can show love by playing a game with someone.** Ask:

- **What are some other ways you can spend time with people and show them love at the same time?**

Say: **You can go to your brother's play at school or you can go to your sister's ballgame. Or you can fix dinner alongside your parent and talk about your day. When we spend time together, we show people we love them.**

Ask the two remaining children to hug or pat each other's backs. **Another way we can show love to others is by giving them a hug or a pat on the back.** Let everyone hug a partner.

Now stand next to the person upfront who represents your favorite way you like to receive love. Give the children a chance to move. **We feel so good when we receive love. God wants us to share that good feeling with everyone around us.**

Open your Bible to Galatians 5:13b-14, and read it. Say: **God wants us to love others. Now stand next to the object that represents how you could share love with someone this week.**

Close in prayer: **Dear God, you show your love for us in so many ways—you gave us a love letter in the Bible, you are always with us, and you gave us the most wonderful gift of your Son, Jesus. Help us know ways to show your love to others. In Jesus' name, amen.**

Medicinal Mirth

Topic: Laughter

Scripture: Proverbs 17:22

Simple Supplies: You'll need a Bible, a book of jokes for children, and an empty bottle of cough syrup.

Say: **I'd like to share a few funny jokes with you.** Read a few jokes from the children's joke book. Invite the children to share a few of their favorite jokes with you. You could also tell a few knock-knock jokes, such as:

Knock, knock!

Who's there?

Hatch.

Hatch who?

God bless you!

Ask:

- **How do you feel when you hear a good joke?**
- **What other kinds of things make you feel happy?**

Hold up the cough syrup bottle, and say: **Did you know that the Bible says a joyful heart is like good medicine? It's true!** Read Proverbs 17:22.

Let's do an experiment that will help us understand why a joyful attitude makes us feel good. Everyone think for a moment about something that makes you feel really crabby and grumpy. Maybe it's when your little sister wants to play with your toys, or maybe it's when you have to do your homework and you'd rather play. Pause. **OK, now everyone laugh out loud for thirty seconds. I'll tell you when to stop. Ready? Go!** Stop them after thirty seconds. Then ask:

- **How did you feel when you were thinking about something that made you crabby?**
- **How did you feel when you were laughing?**
- **Now how do you feel?**

Say: **We feel better when we have a good laugh! Laughter is good medicine! God knows that when we complain, we start seeing only the bad things around us. We can make ourselves "sick" with unhappiness. God wants us to be joyful, to look at the good blessings he's given us, and to spread his joy to everyone.**

Close with prayer: **Dear God, thanks for laughter and what it does for our hearts. Help us use our laughter to show others your love. Amen.**

Have the children laugh as they go back to their seats.

Sum of the Parts

Topic: Gifts

Scripture: Romans 12:4-6a

Simple Supplies: You'll need a Bible, a bright sheet of poster board, and a pair of scissors. Cut the poster board into four large puzzle pieces.

LEADER TIP

For extra impact, have a photo of the church building blown up to a poster-sized print. Build your puzzle from this print. This will help personalize this message for your congregation!

Say: **The Bible says that God gives different spiritual gifts to different people in the church.** Give four children each one piece of the puzzle. **Spiritual gifts are abilities that help people serve the church and make it strong.**

Read Romans 12:4-6a. **The Bible says that we all have different gifts, but we are still one body of Christ—one church. When we work together and use our gifts, we build the church and make it strong. I would like the children who aren't holding puzzle pieces to tell the children with the puzzle pieces where to stand so they can put the puzzle together.**

Give the children a moment to work. Ask:

- **What would have happened if one person wouldn't have shared a puzzle piece with the others?**
- **How is that like what happens if we choose not to share our gifts with others?**
- **What's a gift you can share with the church?**

Say: **God made everyone in the church with different gifts. Some of us are good at welcoming others, some of us can sing, some are great with crafts, and others have big hearts for reaching out to needy people. We all need to share our gifts to make our church strong.**

Ask the puzzle-piece holders to step away from each other. Pray: **Dear God, thank you for giving each of us special gifts.** Next, have the puzzle-piece holders move together in a puzzle shape. **Help us share our gifts to make our church strong. In Jesus' name, amen.**

Stop!

Topic: Repentance

Scripture: Deuteronomy 30:16

Simple Supplies: You'll need a Bible, marker, scissors, and sheet of red poster board. Make a stop sign from the poster board.

Hold up the stop sign and ask kids what it means. Say: **This is a stop sign. When you're driving in the car or riding a bike and you see this sign, you'd better stop or you'll get in trouble. Someone could get hurt!**

When I say "go," everyone stand up and pretend to be driving a car. Stay in this area (motion where you want them to stay), **and "drive" carefully. When you see me hold up the sign, you have to stop. Ready? Go!** Let the kids "drive," and every thirty seconds or so, hold up the stop sign. Make sure they stop! Gather the kids, then ask:

- **What would happen if everyone disobeyed stop signs?**
- **What are some of God's laws?**
- **What happens when we disobey God's laws?**

Say: **We can get hurt or we can hurt others when we disobey stop signs! The same thing happens when we disobey God's laws. We can hurt ourselves and others!**

Open your Bible to Deuteronomy 30:16, and read it out loud. Say: **When we follow God's laws, we know how to live and we know what's right. What a blessing!**

Ask the kids to "drive" again. Every few seconds, hold up the sign, have them stop, then offer a prayer. Continue several times, so several prayers can be said.

End by praying: **Dear God, thank you that you love us so much that you give us rules to keep us safe. In Jesus' name, amen.**

Yummy!

Topic: God's Word

Scripture: Jeremiah 15:16a

Simple Supplies: You'll need a Bible, a washable marker, a wet cloth, and sandwich bags filled with alphabet cereal (one per child).

Open the Bible to Jeremiah 15:16a, and read it to the children: **"When your words came, I ate them; they were my joy and my heart's delight."** Ask:

- **What do you think this verse means?**
- **How does God's Word become a part of us?**

Say: **We really can't eat God's Word, so we have to think about what the Bible is telling us.** Use the marker and write "God's Word" on your hand. **I now have "God's Word" on me, but it's not part of me because I can easily remove it.** Use the wet cloth to remove the marks from your hand, then hold up a Bible.

This is God's Word. Hug the Bible to your chest, then pass it to the person sitting beside you. Have the children each hug the Bible and pass it on as you continue to speak. **The Bible is God's Word. It's close to you when you hug it, but it's not really part of you when it's outside of you.**

LEADER

If you have time, copy the Bible verse on separate slips of paper, and tape a slip to each bag of cereal.

Hold up a bag of alphabet cereal. **Let's think about food. When we eat, food goes inside us. Our body uses food as building blocks to help us grow. When we eat, the food eventually does become part of us. God's Word is like food—it is good for us and as wonderful as a tasty treat.** Ask:

• **How do we get God's Word inside of us so that it can become a part of us?**

Say: **We can read the Bible, think about what God's Word means, pray, sing, and worship. God's Word is awesome! Let's say a prayer to thank God for his Word.**

Pray: **Dear God, thank you for giving us the Bible and for your words in it. Please help us read the Bible, pray, and sing so your words become part of us. In Jesus' name, amen.**

Give each of the children a sandwich bag filled with cereal to help them remember that God's Word, like food, is meant to become part of us.

 Four-year-old Hannah asked, "I asked Jesus into my heart, so when I swallow my food does it hit Jesus' head on the way down?"

No One Knows

Topic: Be Ready

Scripture: Matthew 25:1-13

Simple Supplies: You'll need a Bible, a bottle of bubble solution, and a bubble wand for each child.

LEADER TIP

You can make a bubble wand by straightening the bottom of a large paper clip and bending the top into a triangle (resembling the number four).

Blow a bubble from the bubble mixture. Catch it with the bubble wand and hold it up. If the bubble pops, blow and hold another one on your wand. Say: **Raise your hand when you think this bubble is going to pop. Let's see who can raise a hand closest to the time it pops.** Allow the children to raise their hands. **It's hard to predict when something will happen and hard to wait for it to happen too.**

Open the Bible to Matthew 25:1-13, and show the children the words. Say: **Jesus told a story about some women who were waiting for someone to come so that they could go to a party. They had to wait outside in the dark so they needed lamps to give them light.** Hand out bubble wands. **Pretend you're holding lamps like they did.**

Jesus said that these women didn't know how long they had to wait. Some of them brought extra oil to keep their lamps burning, but some of them didn't bring enough oil. It was really dark outside. Pick up the bubble solution.

I'll blow bubbles and you catch one with your wand. Just sit still in your spot and I'll make sure I send some bubbles your way. You must be careful not to bump the people sitting near you. I only want you to catch one bubble. If it pops, you can't have another, so be careful with your bubble. It's going to be the light for your lamp. Blow small bubbles slowly; catch some for smaller children and hand the bubbles to them. **Let's see how long your "light" lasts.** Play for a while and see whose bubble lasts the longest.

Jesus said that the women without enough oil asked the other women to share. The women with extra oil couldn't share because they didn't know how long they'd have to keep their own lamps lit. So the women without oil left to buy more. They missed the party, because they weren't there when it was time to go.

Jesus told this story because he wants everyone to be ready for when he comes again. We don't know when Jesus will come again. So while we're waiting for him, let's live the way he wants us to, by telling others about him, coming to church, being kind to others, and loving each other. Ask:

- **How can you live like Jesus wants you to?**
- **Who can you tell about Jesus this week?**

Say: **What good ways to live like Jesus wants you to! We never know when Jesus will come, so we need to be ready and live like Jesus. Let's tell everyone about Jesus.**

Blow bubbles and let kids try to catch more. When they catch a bubble, have them say the name of someone they'll tell about Jesus.

Then close in prayer: **Dear God, help us to tell others about Jesus so they can be ready for him to come back too. In his name we pray, amen.**

How Do You Love Me?

Topic: Loving God

Scripture: 1 John 5:3a

Simple Supplies: You'll need a Bible, a small (palm size) paper heart for each child, and rubber bands. Photocopy the "God's Word" handout from page 169 (one for each child). Roll the handouts into scrolls lengthwise, and secure with rubber bands.

Ask:

- **How does God show he loves us?**
- **How do we show we love God?**

Say: **God shows he loves us in so many ways. He gave us his words in the Bible. He gave us Jesus, his Son. He gives us food and families to care for us.**

We can show God we love him by loving others and telling others about Jesus. Listen to what the Bible tells us about loving God. Open your Bible to 1 John 5:3a, and read it out loud. **"This is love for God: to obey his commands." One important way to show God our love is to obey his commands, which are found in the Bible. Let's see what happens when we don't obey.**

Give each child a heart and a Bible handout rolled into a scroll. Say: **Put the paper heart onto your left palm, and bend your fingers down to hold it in place. Now hold your Bible scroll up to your**

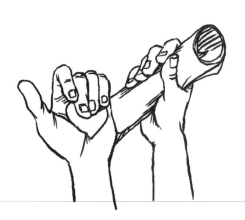

right eye like a telescope. Put the hand holding the heart up against the left side of the scroll at the very end. With both eyes wide open, keep your left hand touching the outside of your scroll, and slide this hand along the left side of the scroll to bring your hand closer to your left eye. The children will notice a "hole" in the heart caused by tunnel vision.

Ask the children what they see. They'll say, "There's a hole in my heart!" Say: **When we don't obey God, we're missing something inside. Our love is not complete unless we both say and show how much we love God. Just like the hole in your paper heart, there's a hole in God's heart, a deep sadness, when we don't act like we love him. Let's pray together.**

Ask the kids to reverse the direction they moved the heart, so that they move it from their left eye back to the end of the scroll. The heart will look complete again. Pray this prayer while they move their hearts: **Dear God, thank you for loving us so much. You've given us many great, wonderful gifts and show us your love each day. Please help us learn how to love you and show you our love. In Jesus' name, amen.**

God's Word

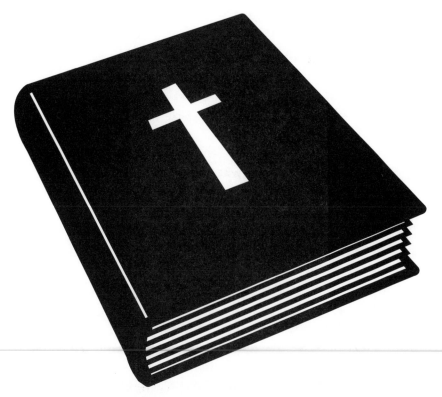

"This is love for God: to obey his commands" (1 John 5:3a).

Permission to photocopy this page from *The Humongous Book of Children's Messages* granted for local church use. Copyright © Group Publishing, Inc., P.O. Box 481, Loveland, CO 80539. www.grouppublishing.com

Help Needed!

Topic: Bullies

Scripture: Proverbs 22:3

Simple Supplies: You'll need a Bible, a bowl, and ice cubes (one for each child).

Say: **I want you to stand when I say the word "bully" and sit when I say "careful." Let's try it. Bully.** Let the children stand. **Careful.** Wait for the children to sit back down. Ask:

- **What is a bully?** Have the children answer standing up.
- **Why should we be careful around them?** Let the children answer after they sit down.

Hand each child a piece of ice. Say: **Hold this piece of ice for now. You may not eat it; just hold it in your hand. You can return your ice cube to the bowl and let go of it whenever you want. I'll read our Bible verse while you hold your ice cubes.**

Show children your Bible, open to Proverbs 22:3. Read aloud: **"A prudent man sees danger and takes refuge, but the simple keep going and suffer for it."**

Our Bible verse says that a smart person finds help when in trouble. Ask:

- **Why do some people decide not to ask for help when they're being bothered by bullies?**

Say: **If you haven't given back your ice cube, please do it now.** Let the children do this. **Just like when you held your ice cubes, you have to decide when to hold on and when to let go of your problem with bullies. We need to ask for help sometimes. It is a smart thing to do. We can ask adults, friends, and especially God to help us.**

Pray: **Dear God, give us wisdom to know when to get help and when to stand up for ourselves. Be with us and let us know that you are near us. We pray for those who pick on us, that you help them change. Thank you for keeping us safe. In Jesus' name, amen.**

Unstuck!

Topics: Sin, Forgiveness

Scripture: Romans 1:29-31; 3:23; 5:8-10

Simple Supplies: You'll need a Bible and two types of stickers—round dots and stars—at least four of each per child.

Give each of the children at least four of each kind of sticker. Say: **We live in a world of stickers! Some stickers are painful and embarrassing...**Put a dot in the middle of your forehead. Say: **While other stickers are promising and encouraging.** Put a star next to it. Ask:

- **What are some good things you've done?** As kids share, say encouraging things like "Great job" and "I knew you could do it." Have all kids stick all their stars on them to represent the good things they've done.

Say: **Wow! That's a lot of good things! Now let's hear some of the bad things the Bible says not to do.** Read Romans 1:29-31, and then say: **This is a long list of bad things! Each time I say one of the bad things, stick a circle dot on you somewhere until you run out of dots. Ready? Greed, jealousy, murder, disobeying parents, being mean, being proud.**

Pause while kids stick all their dots on them.

Say: **That's a long list of what God doesn't want his people to do. Some are *real* bad things like murder. But did you notice that in this same list are things like disobeying your parents, being proud, and just being mean? I think most of us have done those three things at one time or another.**

Read aloud Romans 3:23: **The Bible tells us that "all have sinned and fall short of the glory of God." We've all missed the mark.**

We are quite the sticky mess, aren't we? The stars are nice, but the dots are what really hurt. But here's one of the greatest truths in the Bible: We don't have to live with our dots of sin. We can let Jesus have them. When we ask Jesus to forgive us, he will remove the dots of sin. It's because Jesus loves us so much!

Read Romans 5:8-10, then go to the children and start removing the dots and stars. Say: **Did you notice that God doesn't just take your "dots," but he also takes the "stars"? Everything you do— good or bad—is for God. He will remove the bad, and use the good for his glory.**

Place the stickers in a pile, and have the children join hands around it. Close in a prayer: **Dear God, we are so thankful that because of Jesus, our sins are taken away. We want you to know that we want all of our good things to help people see and learn about you. In Jesus' name, amen.**

I Love You

Topic: Love Each Other

Scripture: 1 John 4:20-21

Simple Supplies: You'll need a Bible.

Say: **Let's play a game to learn more about each other. I'll say a way for you to form a group, and you find others who are like you to make a group.** Try these ideas and others.

- **Group according to your favorite pizza topping—cheese, pepperoni, sausage.** Motion where the three different groups will stand.
- **Group according to the number of people in your family.** Motion where children should stand if there are two or three family members, four or five family members, or six or more family members. And pets don't count!
- **Group according to whether you are boys or girls.**

After each grouping, have the kids say to one another in their group: "God loves you and so do I."

After the game, ask:

- **Is it easy or hard for you to tell others "I love you"? Why?**

Say: **We're sometimes uncomfortable when we say "I love you," aren't we?**

Listen to what the Bible says about love. Read aloud 1 John 4:19-21, then say: **God loves you no matter what group you find yourself in. And when we love another person in God's name, we're not just loving God but actually showing God to that person.**

Have everyone pray together out loud: "We love you, God!"

Close by praying: **Dear God, thanks for your love. Help us to love those around us, no matter what group we are in.**

Let It Go

Topic: Following Jesus

Scripture: Matthew 19:16-22

Simple Supplies: You'll need a Bible, two plastic one-gallon milk cartons, small toys, candy, scissors, and duct tape.

Cut off the tops of the two cartons so the hole is just large enough for a small child to get his or her hand into it. Cover each hole's edges with duct tape so kids don't scratch their wrists when they reach in. Fill one carton with small toys and the other carton with wrapped candy.

Show the children the two prepared cartons of goodies. Invite them to come forward and get a treasure or treat. Several things might happen. Some children might be too shy to come get a goody. Some might reach into the carton, grab lots of goodies, then not be able to get their hands back out of the hole. Others' hands might not fit in the first place. Ask:

- **What did you do when I asked you to come get a treasure or treat?** You'll get a variety of responses.
- **Who had trouble trying to get the treats out of the carton? What did you have to do?**

Say: **All kinds of things happened to us! Some of us didn't want to try. Some of us couldn't even get into the cartons. Some of us grabbed too much and had to let go. That's like in life. Some people don't have any treats. Some are content with just a little. Some have so much that they can't let go.**

Read Matthew 19:16-22.

Say: **The Bible tells about a man who had many riches. He was a young man who claimed to be a good person. Jesus told him to sell his things, give the money away, and follow Jesus. The man didn't want to let go of any of his riches. The young man walked away instead.** Ask the children to hold both hands out with palms up. Instruct the children to say, each time you pause, "Jesus, we give it to you."

- **Our hands may be full of activities, like baseball or soccer or clubs.** Pause for kids to say, "Jesus, we give it to you."
- **Our hands may be full of friends that may influence us to do things that aren't what you want.** Pause for kids to say, "Jesus, we give it to you."
- **Our hands may be full of fears that keep us from doing the right thing or following you.** Pause for kids to say, "Jesus, we give it to you."
- **Our hands may be full of trouble that we simply can't outrun.** Pause for kids to say, "Jesus, we give it to you."
- **Our hands may be full of expectations that we try to live up to. We try to do and be somebody we aren't.** Pause for kids to say, "Jesus, we give it to you."

Jesus, we have empty hands right now. Use us. Fill our empty hands with your love and purpose. Give us your work. We love you and want to follow you. In your name, amen.

Running the Race

Topic: Following Jesus

Scripture: 1 Corinthians 9:24-27

Simple Supplies: You'll need a Bible.

Read aloud 1 Corinthians 9:24-27. Then ask the children to stand and spread their arms out, like a cross. Instruct the children to leave their arms up throughout the message. Say: **There are many races a person can run. Some races, like the Boston Marathon, are many miles long, while other races are what we call sprints—short, fast races of limited distance. The one-hundred–yard dash. The fifty-meter race. There are many races in life, but only one that counts. It's a race to a finish line that may be years down the road. We don't know when. It's called the race of life.** Encourage the kids to run in place (with arms extended) for thirty seconds, then stop—but keep their arms extended like a cross.

The Apostle Paul knew all about running races. He lived and worked among people who enjoyed going to athletic events and races. They had their heroes, just like we do. Ask:

- **Who has ever been in a race at a track meet or at a field day? How did you do?**
- **What do you need to do to race your best?**

Say: **When we race, we keep our eyes on the goal. We run with all of our energy and enthusiasm to the finish line. Sometimes we might feel like giving up.**

Let the kids place their arms around each other's shoulders. Say: **Ahhhhhh. We need to remember that in our race for Jesus, we don't have to go it alone. We have friends to help us.**

Tell the kids to keep their arms around each other as you pray: **Dear God, help us help each other in this race of life. Help us keep our eyes focused on Jesus and run the race the best we can for you! In Jesus' name, amen.**

Molding for the Future

Topic: Parents

Scripture: Proverbs 1:8-9

Simple Supplies: You'll need a Bible, modeling dough (a handful for each child), and waxed paper.

Give each child a sheet of waxed paper to work on and a handful of modeling dough. Tell the children to mold a shape of what they'd like to be doing in the future. For example, they could mold a soccer ball if they want to be a soccer coach, they could mold a book if they want to be a teacher, they could mold a truck if they want to be a firefighter. After the models are complete, invite children to share their creations with the others. Ask:

- **How easy or hard was it to mold your piece of clay into what you wanted to do or become? Why?**

Say: **One of the most difficult, yet rewarding, modeling jobs in the world is molding another person. This is what your parents get to do! God has given them the special work of molding you into a person who honors him, treats others with kindness and respect, and understands the ways of life.**

Read Proverbs 1:8-9, then ask:

- **What are some important things your parents have taught you so far?**
- **How will those teachings help you when you are an adult?**
- **How can you show appreciation and honor to your parents this week?**

Say: **Our parents help us learn how to treat our families and friends. They try their hardest to mold us into the adults we will one day become. Let's show them we appreciate them by helping them with chores, by doing our homework without whining, and by telling them we love them!**

Ask the children to hold their models as you pray: **God, we ask that you help us honor our parents this week. Give us ideas for** helping them. **Help us not to do things that might frustrate them. Help us to honor them, for we know that's what you want. We love you, God. In Jesus' name, amen.**

Spread the News

Topic: Sharing Faith

Scripture: Matthew 28:19-20

Simple Supplies: You'll need a Bible, a toothbrush, a glass, individually wrapped candy, a video game, and a box to put everything in.

Say: **Today we're going to talk about sharing. I'll take several items out of this box. You tell me if it's a good idea to share the item with others or not.** Pull out the video game (cool to share), pull out the toothbrush (*gross,* don't share), pull out the wrapped candy (great idea to share at the end of the message), pull out the glass (*gross,* don't share), and finally pull out the Bible (a definite "yes" to share).

Open your Bible to Matthew 28:19-20, and read it to the children. Ask:

- **What does Jesus want us to do?**
- **How can we share Jesus' love?**
- **Who can you tell about Jesus?**

Say: **The Bible is the best of things to share with others. Jesus wants us to tell others about how much God loves them. God wants everyone to know that they'll live forever with him.**

Close by praying: **God, please give us the courage to share our faith in Jesus. What a great thing to share. Thank you for giving us such a wonderful gift. In his name we pray, amen.**

Share the wrapped candy with everyone.

JER333

Topic: Prayer

Scripture: Jeremiah 33:3

Simple Supplies: You'll need a Bible, a baseball mitt, a chair, a volunteer to play "Joey," and another volunteer to play "Mom" offstage. Rehearse the skit prior to the message.

Gather the children, and invite them to enjoy the message show.

(Joey enters and searches everywhere for his baseball mitt, which is lying under a chair, he just doesn't notice it. Mom is offstage.)

Joey: **Mom, can you help me find my baseball mitt? I've looked everywhere! Even in the trash can!**

Mom: **Have you tried your closet?** (Pause, while Joey pantomimes looking in a closet, then shaking his head.) **Have you checked behind the door?** (Pause while Joey pantomimes looking behind a door.)

Joey: **Mom! I didn't find it! Do you have any more ideas?**

Mom: **Hmm. Try looking under your chair.** (Joey does, and finds it!)

Joey: **Hey! I found it!** (Joey lifts the mitt high.) **Thanks, Mom! You know everything! You're the best!** (Joey exits.)

Ask:

- **How was Joey talking to his mom like us talking to God?**
- **Could Joey see his mom? Did that stop him from calling out to her?**
- **Can we see God? Does that stop us from calling out to him?**

Say: **Joey knew his mom was in the other room, and he knew his mom would help him.**

We can't see God, but we know he's always there for us. There's a number you can use to get in touch with God. You can use it any time, even in emergencies. The number is not 9-1-1. The number is JER333. It stands for the book of Jeremiah, chapter 33, verse 3. Open your Bible to Jeremiah 33:3, and read it out loud. **"Call to me and I will answer you and tell you great and unsearchable things you do not know."**

Even though we can't see God, we know he's there for us. God talks to us through the Bible, through Christian friends, and through the church. He wants us to call on him and know that he's always there for us.

Call on God right now by saying a prayer. Have the children pretend to dial and talk on a phone while you pray. **Dear God, thank you for being there for us when we call on you. Please hear us as we tell you what we're thankful for.** Let kids pray. **In Jesus' name, amen.**

Name That Talent

Topic: Talents

Scripture: Colossians 3:23-24

Simple Supplies: You'll need a Bible, a basketball, sheet music, and an instrument. Hide the items in a box or basket until you need them. Ask a child ahead of time to say the closing prayer.

Say: **Hello and welcome to "Name That Talent." Today I have a few objects that are used by some very talented kids. You will have a chance to hear and see some clues before you try to "name that talent."**

Are you ready for the first set of clues? Let the children respond. Help them to be excited about the game! **Let us begin with the first set of clues:**

- **Many people gather in a gym to watch this.**
- **You use your hands, feet, and eyes to do this.**

Give kids a chance to guess before you pull out the basketball. Say: **OK, here's a clue for you to see.** Bring out the basketball, and let kids guess. **Someone who plays basketball must be athletic. The talent is "athletic."**

Now for talent number two! The next set of clues is:

- **Many people who do this can read, but they don't read words.**
- **You need to know the difference between loud and soft, fast and slow, and when to start and stop.**

Give kids a chance to guess. Say: **OK, here's a clue for you to see.** Bring out the instrument and sheet music, and let kids guess. **Who can name that talent? A person who can play an instrument must be musical. The talent is called "musical."** Ask:

- **What other talents are there?**
- **What talents do you have?**

Open your Bible to Colossians 3:23, and show the children the words. Say: **The Bible says to do whatever we do as though we're doing it for the Lord, not for people. All of us are good at something. We just have to figure out what that something is. We might not be musical or athletic, but maybe we have the talent of making people laugh, or making friends easily, or sharing our faith with others. Whatever talent we have, we need to use it as if we are doing it for God. He's our best fan.**

Call up the child you asked ahead of time to say the closing prayer. Say: [Name of child], **one of your talents is sharing your faith and saying wonderful prayers. Pray for us now, and we'll all be doing it for the Lord.**

After the child prays, have everyone join you in saying: **In Jesus' name, amen.**

Variety Is the Spice of Life

Topic: Worship

Scripture: John 4:23-24

Simple Supplies: You'll need a Bible, a CD player, and a CD with a fast worship song and a slow worship song. Any familiar songs will work.

Say: **Did you know that there are many ways to worship Jesus? Not everyone is the same, so we have many ways of showing our love for him and worshipping him. Sometimes we get really excited. We are more active in our worship. We may clap our hands, sing loudly, and raise our hands toward heaven. We may even dance as we sing to the Lord.** Play the fast worship song, and let kids clap, sing along, raise their hands, and dance.

Then there are times when we worship quietly. We may sit still and think about Jesus. We sing softly and sometimes bow our heads in worship. Play the slow worship song, and let the kids bow their heads, sing quietly, and fold their hands in prayer.

Open your Bible to John 4:23-24, and show the words to the children. Say: **The Bible says that God is looking for people who worship in spirit and truth. No matter what way we worship, we need to do it with love in our hearts. We are worshipping in spirit and truth if we're doing it to praise God who loves us.** Ask:

LEADER TIP

If you have time, you could ask the children to act out these verses that show us a variety of ways to worship.

- Exodus 34:8: "Moses bowed to the ground at once and worshiped."
- Psalm 46:10: "Be still, and know that I am God; I will be exalted among the nations, I will be exalted in the earth."
- Psalm 47:1: "Clap your hands, all you nations; shout to God with cries of joy."
- Psalm 95:6: "Come, let us bow down in worship, let us kneel before the Lord our Maker."
- Psalm 134:2: "Lift up your hands in the sanctuary and praise the Lord."

- **What is your favorite thing to do when you worship?**
- **Why do you want to worship?**

Say: **We may like different ways to worship, depending on our day and how we feel. I just love to worship because I love Jesus. I want Jesus to know how much I love him!**

Let's worship God through prayer. Ask for volunteers to pray.

Close with this prayer: **God, I want to worship you in truth and prayer. I love you, and I know these children do too! In Jesus' name, amen.**

At the end of a message, Pastor Greg led kids in singing the praise song "Great Is the Lord Almighty." One adult overheard a little three-year-old girl singing, "Greg is the Lord Almighty."

Shake, Rattle, and Roll

Topic: Praise

Scripture: Luke 19:37-40

Simple Supplies: You'll need a Bible, a handful of pebbles and stones in a plastic bowl, and a lid for the bowl.

Open your Bible to Luke 19, and show the children the words. Say: **When Jesus entered Jerusalem riding a donkey, the whole crowd began to joyfully shout praises for all the miracles they'd seen. The people were shouting praises such as "Blessed is the king who comes in the name of the Lord!" When some others in the crowd heard the shouting, they told Jesus to make the people stop. Jesus had a surprising answer: "I tell you, if they keep quiet, the stones will cry out."**

Bring out the bowl of pebbles and stones, and ask:

- **What do you think Jesus meant about the stones being able to praise him if the people were kept quiet?**

Hold the bowl up to your ear. Let others "listen" to the stones. Ask if anyone hears anything.

Say: **Jesus is the Lord of all creation. All creation praises him. If people are silent, the stones will cry out in praise. Maybe someday we'll actually get to see all creation joining in praising Jesus the king. Wouldn't that be awesome? In the meantime, let's use this container of stones to help us praise Jesus.**

Cover the bowl with the lid, then shake it like a maraca. Let kids take turns shaking the bowl of stones while they say a praise like "Thanks for loving me!" or "You are the most awesome Savior" or "I'll love you forever!"

Close in a praise prayer: **You truly are wonderful, Jesus, and I want to praise you forever. In your name, amen.**

Focus on God

Topic: Distractions

Scripture: Deuteronomy 6:5

Simple Supplies: You'll need a Bible, a soccer ball, pen, and sticky notes.

Toss the soccer ball up and down as you call kids forward for the message. Ask:

- **How many of you play soccer or another sport? How many of you have watched a soccer game?**
- **What do you need to do if you want to score a goal?**

Say: **Many people like soccer and love watching the game. A couple of things I know about playing soccer and scoring are that you have to watch what you're doing, keep your eye on where you're going, and be determined and enthusiastic. When it's time to kick the ball into the goal, you have to watch where you're kicking and go for it!**

Bring out the sticky notes. Hold up the soccer ball and say: **Pretend this ball is you and me.** Ask two kids to stand several feet away and hold their arms like a soccer goal. **Pretend the goal is God and our relationship with him.** Ask:

- **What kinds of things might distract us from keeping our eyes on the goal and winning some points for our soccer team?** Answers could be "too much yelling from parents," "not keeping our eyes on the ball," or "an animal or another soccer ball coming onto the field."
- **What kinds of things might distract us from keeping our eyes on God?** Answers could be "too many things to do," "wrong friends,"

"not taking time to read the Bible," and so on. Write the answers kids give you on the sticky notes, and stick them to the soccer ball. Continue until the soccer ball is covered with sticky notes, then hold it high.

Say: **What a lot of distractions. If I were playing a soccer game, I could never score a goal with this ball. If this were me in life, I'd have a really tough time focusing on God! Let's pray and give our distractions to God.**

Pray: **Dear God, we give our distractions to you. We give you** [name the distractions as you take off the sticky notes]. **We're sorry that we don't place you first in our lives. Help us to always keep our eyes on you. In Jesus' name, amen.** Toss the distraction-free ball up and down as you tell kids to go back to their seats.

Changing Colors

Topic: Sharing Faith

Scripture: Luke 19:28-40; 23:1-49

Simple Supplies: You'll need a Bible, a chameleon, a box of sand, and green leaves or a light green bedsheet or piece of poster board.

LEADER

Ask the children ahead of time who has a chameleon you could borrow for the message. Or go to a pet store and buy or borrow the supplies.

Start out with the chameleon in the sand. Show the children what you brought, then say: **Look at this chameleon! Chameleons are able to do something that most other animals can't. What do you think that might be?** Pause while kids respond. **Chameleons are able to change their color depending on their surroundings. If they're in a dark green forest, they turn dark green. If they're in the sand, they turn tan. I'll show you what I mean.**

Place the green leaves all around the chameleon. It'll take a couple minutes for the chameleon to change colors. While you're waiting, bring out your Bible, and show the children Luke 19:28-40. Say: **Sometimes people are like the chameleon. We might act a certain way with one group of friends, then change colors with another group of friends. Maybe we act one way at church, then act another way at school or work.**

Well, Jesus faced this same chameleon-like attitude. When he rode the donkey colt into Jerusalem, everyone cheered because of all the miracles he'd done. The people wanted him to be king! Then, when Jesus did what God wanted instead of what the people wanted, the people got angry and their "chameleon" hearts changed colors. The people who had cheered for Jesus changed! They didn't stand up for Jesus when crowds of people wanted him crucified.

Show kids the chameleon that has changed colors because of the new surroundings. Ask:

- **What did the people in the story do that was wrong?**
- **How can we do what's right no matter if we are at church, school, or home?**

Say: **The people in the story didn't stand up for Jesus. At first they cheered for him, then they were against him. No matter what our surroundings are, we need to stand up for Jesus and tell people how much he loves them. Whether we are at church or at school or at home, let's stay strong and tell people about Jesus.**

Ask the children to join hands for prayer. **Dear God, no matter where we are—at church, school, or home—help us always do what's right. If we know something is wrong, help us stand up and not go along with the crowd. Thanks for Jesus who died for us and forgives us. Thanks for your unchanging love for us. In Jesus' name, amen.**

What a Load

Topics: Sin, Forgiveness

Scripture: Psalm 103:12

Simple Supplies: You'll need a Bible, a robe for "Jesus," and a wheelbarrow filled with heavy bricks. Ask another person to be "Jesus" and take your heavy load from you during the message.

Struggle to push the wheelbarrow toward the children, and talk as you push: **Man, I have a heavy load here. Actually, I've been thinking about some things I need to ask forgiveness for. I think that's why this load feels so heavy. There are times I've not been very nice to my neighbors.**

Pick up a brick, put it back in the wheelbarrow, then struggle to push the wheelbarrow again. **I've said some bad things I wish I wouldn't have.**

Pick up a brick, put it back in the wheelbarrow, then struggle to push the wheelbarrow again. **And I have a huge grudge against someone who hurt me.**

Pick up a brick, put it back in the wheelbarrow, then struggle to push the wheelbarrow again. Encourage some children to try to help you push it. Pause a moment to wipe your brow. Ask:

• **What are some things you're sorry for?**

Let each of the children name something, then pick up a brick and put it back in the wheelbarrow. Then say: **We need to pray to Jesus and ask him to forgive us. We need help with this heavy load.**

Ask the children to close their eyes as you pray. Have "Jesus" enter during the prayer and come to you and the wheelbarrow. **Dear Jesus, we're sorry for the bad things we've done. We feel heavy with guilt. Please forgive us. In your precious name, amen.**

Ask the kids to open their eyes. Then have "Jesus" take the handles of the wheelbarrow and exit with the burden. Open your Bible to Psalm 103:12, and say: **"As far as the east is from the west, so far** has he removed our transgressions from us." That means when Jesus forgives us, he removes our sin forever. Amen!

A leader used a globe to highlight different countries in the world. The topic was "God Loves Everyone—All Around the World." When the leader asked if any of the kids had ever traveled to another country, he got answers such as France, Canada, and Italy. But one little girl said that she and her family had recently gone to the country of "Bufay." The leader wasn't familiar with that country so he inquired again thinking that he just didn't understand her correctly. At that, her mother, who was nearby, whispered sheepishly, "She means Country Buffet—the restaurant."

Sending God Flowers

Topic: Sharing Faith

Scripture: Matthew 25:40

Simple Supplies: You'll need a Bible, a men's shirt in a gift box, several boxes of cereal in a grocery bag, and a bouquet of flowers.

Say: **Lately I've been thinking about how much God has done for us. He created each of us to be unique. There's no one else like us. He's given us homes, food, and families. He watches over us and guides our lives. The best thing God gave us is his Son, Jesus, who died on the cross so we could live forever. Jesus loves us better than anyone on earth can love us. When I think of all he's done, my heart overflows with love for him!**

So I decided to show God how much I love him. I bought him some presents. Just as I give gifts to people I love, I thought I'd give some to God, too! First, I bought him a shirt. Remove the shirt from its box, and hold it up.

Do you think he'll like the color? I wonder if I got the right size. Allow kids to express their thoughts about your gift. Return the shirt to the box, and take out the grocery bag with cereal.

Then I bought God some cereal. Show the different kinds. **I didn't know what kind God likes best, so I bought several kinds!**

Bring out the bouquet of flowers. **How about flowers? If I send God flowers, he'll really know how much I love him!** Allow kids to respond. Ask:

- **Could God really use these gifts?**
- **How else could I show God I love him?**

Say: **Although it's a really thoughtful idea to give God these kinds of gifts, he doesn't really need a shirt or cereal or a bouquet. God can see in my heart, and he knows I love him. But there is an important way I can show God I love him.**

Open the Bible, and read Matthew 25:40. Say: **The Bible says "Whatever you did for one of the least of these brothers of mine, you did for me." That means when we reach out and help people who might go unnoticed or who seem unimportant to others, we're doing it for God. So the shirt idea would be a good one if I gave it to someone who needs a shirt.** Ask kids to offer ideas of people who might need shirts.

We can help the poor, who are often forgotten by others. The cereal and the bouquet might go well at our outreach center in town. Or mention another place in town you could take the flowers.

When we offer these gifts of love to others, it's as if we were giving them to Jesus.

As we pray, think of someone you could show love to as if you were doing it for Jesus. Pray silently for that person. Pray: **Dear God, you love us so much, and we want to love you in return. Help us show our love to you by doing a loving thing for...**(pause for children to pray). **Help them feel your love through us. In Jesus' name, amen.**

Showing God Your Homework

Topics: School, Homework

Scripture: Colossians 3:23

Simple Supplies: You'll need a Bible, two sheets of poster board, and markers. Prepare one poster with a simple, neat drawing. Scribble on the second poster, and tear the edges so it looks really messy.

Say: **All of us either go to school or know someone who goes to school, right?** Pause. **Well, we go to school to learn things like reading and writing. Sometimes we have homework, which could be writing a story, drawing a picture to go along with a story, or finishing math problems.** Ask:

- **Who checks your homework when you finish it?**
- **Is there anyone else who looks at your homework?**

Say: **Usually either your teacher or a parent checks your homework, sometimes both! You learn what they expect, and you do your homework to please them. Someone else is interested in your homework. Someone you might not have thought about...God is interested.** Ask:

- **Have you ever shown your homework to God?**
- **Do you ever think of him watching you do your homework?**

Say: **God is with us all the time. He's there when we're at school, and he's there at home when we're working on homework.**

Open your Bible to Colossians 3:23, and read it. Say: **The Bible says that whatever we do, we need to do our best, as if we were working for the Lord, not for people!**

Show the two posters side by side. Ask:

- **Which of these posters looks like it was made by someone who was doing his or her best?**
- **How can you tell?**

Say: **God understands our work may not be perfect. He knows we'll make mistakes. The great thing about showing God our homework is he always loves and accepts us. He knows some of our work is easy and some is hard. Sometimes we make a few mistakes, and sometimes we make many. God's love for us will not change. When we ask for his help to do our best, God is pleased.**

Homework is not the only work we can do for God. If you help at your house by picking up toys, setting the table, or cleaning your room, you can do your best for God.

Pray: **Dear God, when we do our work, whether at school or at home, help us work with all our heart. Help us remember we're doing our best for you, because you gave your best for us, your Son Jesus. In Jesus' name, amen.**

God Goes With You!

Topic: Facing Fears

Scripture: Deuteronomy 31:6

Simple Supplies: You'll need a Bible and something that represents security (such as a blanket, well-loved stuffed animal, or favorite pillow).

Say: **When I was very young, I was afraid to ride the school bus. Not everyone is afraid of the bus. Some kids love it! But I was afraid. The bus stop was a long way from my house, and I didn't have any friends to wait with me. I worried I might miss the bus or that the bus wouldn't come.** Substitute another appropriate childhood fear if you didn't fear riding a school bus. Ask:

- **What are you afraid of?**
- **What do you do when you're afraid?**

Bring out the security item, and hold it close. Say: **Everyone feels afraid sometimes, although something that scares you may not scare your friend. Something that makes your friend afraid may not bother you. Some people have a special blanket or toy that gives them security at night when they go to sleep.**

Open your Bible to Deuteronomy 31:6, and say: **Listen to what the Bible says for us to do when we're afraid. "Be strong and courageous. Do not be afraid or terrified because of them, for the Lord your God goes with you; he will never leave you nor forsake you."**

When I was afraid while I waited for the school bus, someone was with me all the time. I just didn't know it! God was with me. Since we can't see God, it's easy to forget he's with us, especially when we're afraid. Let's practice remembering that God is always with us!

Close your eyes, and let's pretend we're waiting for the bus. Wait while children settle and close their eyes, then continue: **Maybe we're feeling a little worried or lonely, but remember, God is waiting for the bus with us! While we wait with God, we can talk to him about our school, our friends, anything! When the bus comes, we can pretend to hold God's hand and climb up the steps together. Do you think God would smile as he helped us on? Then we can pretend that God is sitting next to us. Even though we can't see God, we can remember that he's with us wherever we go.** Ask the children to open their eyes.

Let's learn to cheer this Bible verse to help us remember God is with us. Pat your legs in rhythm saying, "God goes with me!" Then clap your hands saying, "He never leaves me!" Demonstrate for the kids, then have kids join in. Repeat the cheer several times, getting louder each time.

Pray: **Dear God, thank you for caring about our fears. Whenever we're afraid, help us pretend to hold your hand. Remind us that "God goes with us, he never leaves us!" In Jesus' name, amen.**

Imitate God

Topic: Honesty

Scripture: Ephesians 5:1; Hebrews 6:18

Simple Supplies: You'll need a Bible.

Open your Bible to Ephesians 5:1, and read it to the kids. Say: **The Bible says we're supposed to imitate God like dearly loved children. God loves us and wants us to be like him. Before we talk more about imitating God, I think we need a little imitating practice. When I tell you to imitate or act like a certain thing, you do it! Ready?**

Ask the children to stand and act out several animals as you name them, such as monkeys, chickens, and bears. Then ask the children to sit again.

Say: **As I watched, I could tell you were imitating a monkey, chicken, or bear because you were saying and doing things those animals would say or do.**

God wants us to imitate him. We can say things he'd say and do things he'd do. When we imitate God, we show others what God is like. Ask:

- **What are some things God would say?**
- **What are some things God would do?**

Say: **God tells us about his love for us in the Bible. We can imitate God and tell others, too. God cares for us by giving us family, friends, our church, and other Christians. We can imitate God by caring for others and always treating people with kindness.**

Open your Bible to Hebrews 6:18, then say: **The Bible says that God always tells the truth. We can trust that he'll keep all his promises. God will never mislead or trick us. God never lies. In fact, it's impossible for God to lie! OK, imitate me as I remind you of this lesson.**

Raise your arms high, then say: **Always imitate God.** Ask the children to repeat your actions and the sentence.

Place both hands side by side, like a book, then say: **Tell people God's words in the Bible.** Ask the children to repeat your actions and the sentence.

Hug a child and say: **Treat others with love and care.** Ask kids to repeat.

Put a finger to your lips, then say: **Don't lie.** Ask kids to repeat.

Give a thumbs-up sign, then say: **Always tell the truth.** Ask kids to repeat.

Close with a prayer: **Dear God, you are good and loving. Help all of us imitate you in all our words and actions.**

Forever With Jesus

Topic: Death

Scripture: John 11:1-45

Simple Supplies: You'll need a Bible and a roll of toilet tissue.

Open your Bible to John 11, and show the children the words. Say: **Our Bible story for today is about Jesus raising Lazarus from the dead. Before I tell you more of the story, I need two volunteers.** Ask your volunteers to wrap you up in toilet tissue by unrolling the roll around you as you continue with the story.

In Jesus' day, when people died and were buried, they were wrapped in strips of cloth. Let's imagine that I'm Lazarus being wrapped in cloth. People who died were placed in a tomb, and a rock was rolled in front to block the entrance. How are you doing, cloth wrappers? Keep up the good work!

Lazarus' two sisters—Mary and Martha—were crying because they missed their brother. Jesus joined them in crying because Jesus loved Lazarus too. Jesus came to the tomb and asked for the stone in front of the tomb to be taken away. Jesus prayed,

then said: **"Lazarus, come out!"** Make sure you are wrapped as much as possible with the toilet tissue.

OK, on the count of three, all of you say: "Lazarus, come out!" Ready? One, two, three! Lead kids in shouting, "Lazarus, come out!" As kids say the words, break out of the wrapping. **Lazarus walked out of the tomb! Jesus brought Lazarus to life again!** Ask:

- **How did Mary and Martha feel at the beginning of the story? at the end of the story?**
- **How do you feel when someone you love dies?**
- **What do you think you'll like about living forever with Jesus in heaven?**

Say: **We're sad when someone we love dies, just as Mary and Martha were sad because their brother died. They were so happy when Jesus brought him to life again. When Jesus died and rose again, he beat death forever. When we feel sad when someone dies, we need to trust in Jesus' grace and love. We can look forward to living forever with Jesus in heaven.**

Ask the kids to each hold onto some of the tissue "cloths" as you pray: **Dear God, thanks for giving Jesus power to raise people to live forever. Thanks for heaven and eternal life. In Jesus' name, amen.**

Rock Solid

Topic: Faith

Scripture: Hebrews 11:1

Simple Supplies: You'll need a Bible.

Say: **The Bible tells us about many men and women who had a strong faith even in difficult situations or tough times. When we want to describe something as really strong, we can use the words "rock solid." So today, when we talk about these people,**

I'll tell you when to say those words and do the motions. For the word *rock,* **pound your fist into your other palm. For the word** *solid,* **punch your fist in the air. Let's try it.** Practice the words and the motions a few times.

Open your Bible to Hebrews 11:1, and show the children the words. Say: **The Bible says, "Now faith is being sure of what we hope for and certain of what we do not see." When Noah was warned about the flood, he had faith and built the ark. Noah's faith was rock solid.** Lead kids in the words and actions for "rock solid."

When Abraham was told to go to a new place, he had faith and went! Abraham's faith was rock solid. Lead kids in the words and actions.

When Moses was told to save God's people and bring them to a new land, he had faith and went! Moses' faith was rock solid. Lead kids in the words and actions.

Those are just a few of the people the Bible tells us about who had rock solid faith. Ask:

• **Who do you know today who has faith?**

After kids name several teachers, pastors, family members, or themselves, say: **God has placed all these Christians in our lives. Their faith is rock solid.** Lead kids in the words and actions.

Pray: **Dear God, thanks for all the people who believe in the Bible, for all the Christians you've placed in our lives today, and for each child present. Thank you for your forgiveness, and thank you for your strength. Please help us keep our faith rock solid.** Have kids repeat the words and actions. **In Jesus' name, amen.**

Sweet Sounds of Praise

Topic: Praise

Scripture: Matthew 21:14-16

Simple Supplies: You'll need a Bible and treats that will turn children's mouths and lips different colors, such as colored candy or frozen pops. Choose a familiar praise chorus to have the children sing at the end of this message.

Say: **I just love kids and you brighten my day each time I see you. Jesus loved kids too. In fact, he said that children are very, very important.** Open your Bible to Matthew 21:14-16, and show the kids the words. **I'm going to give each of you a treat to eat as I read these verses.** Pass out the colorful treats, then read the verses while the kids eat.

"The blind and the lame came to [Jesus] at the temple, and he healed them. But when the chief priests and the teachers of the law saw the wonderful things he did and the children shouting in the temple area, 'Hosanna to the Son of David,' they were indignant. 'Do you hear what these children are saying?' they asked him. 'Yes,' replied Jesus, 'have you never read, "From the lips of children and infants you have ordained praise"?' "

Wow! Jesus told those adults that kids are important, especially when it comes to praise. When you sing praises to God, he wants you to know that what you're doing is special. You're helping others see that God is important to you! Ask:

- **How do you feel knowing Jesus thinks you're so important?**
- **How can you praise him?**

Say: **Jesus loves you so much! It makes us want to praise him always. Let's sing a praise chorus together. As we face the congregation, I'd like everyone to notice these children's lips. They're colorfully standing out so everyone will know that the praises they offer to God are important!**

Close with prayer: **Dear Jesus, thank you for these children and their praises to you. Help all of us remember to praise you, for you are worthy of all our praise. In your name, amen.**

Brightly Lit Path

Topic: Good Choices

Scripture: Psalm 119:105

Simple Supplies: You'll need a Bible and a small flashlight.

Ask:

- **When you get up in the morning, what choices do you make?**
- **When you're at school, what choices do you make? at home?**

Say: **Choices, choices. We get up and choose what to wear and what to eat. We go to school and choose whether or not to listen to the teacher, or to be nice to a new kid. We go home and we have to choose whether or not to be kind to our brother or sister. So many choices.** Ask:

- **How do you know whether a choice is good or bad?**

Say: **A bad choice would hurt others and hurt yourself. Close your eyes for a minute, and think about a bad choice you've made. Maybe you've been mean to a neighbor. Maybe you told a lie.** While kids' eyes are closed, open the Bible to Psalm 119:105, turn on the flashlight, and lay it on the opened Bible.

When we need to make difficult choices, the Bible can give us a clear,

LEADER

Go to a local discount store, and purchase a glow stick for each child. At the end of the message, say: **As you leave today, I have a light for you—a glow stick. Remember that when you're faced with making a tough choice, you can turn to the light, God's Word, for help, and God will help you make a good choice.**

lighted path to the right choice. Go ahead and open your eyes. Psalm 119:105 says, "Your word is a lamp to my feet and a light for my path."

Have the children hold their hands together in front of them, palms up, like a book. Say: **As I shine the light on your hands, think about a verse from the Bible that helps you make good decisions. And think about a decision that you need to make today.** Slowly shine the light on the hands of each child.

Close by shining the flashlight on the Bible and praying: **Dear God, thank you for your Word that shows us the right choices to make and the right way to live our lives. Thanks for forgiveness when we make wrong choices. Thanks most of all for Jesus. In Jesus' name, amen.**

Faithfully Certain

Topic: Faith

Scripture: Hebrews 11:1

Simple Supplies: You'll need a Bible, a kernel of corn, a husk of corn, and candy corn.

Hold up the kernel of corn, and say: **Take a look at this kernel of corn.** Ask:

- **What would happen if we planted this kernel of corn?**

Say: **Even though this kernel of corn doesn't look like much, it could grow into a cornstalk. We have faith that the seed will produce more corn.** Bring out the husk of corn. **Take a look at this husk.** Ask:

- **What do you think is inside the husk?**
- **How do you know that there's corn in the husk if you haven't peeked inside?**

Say: **Having faith is like knowing that this husk has an ear of corn in it. Even though we can't see the corn, we trust that the little seed like we saw earlier produced what it was supposed to. Let's take a look.** Open the husk, and show children the ear of corn.

Open your Bible to Hebrews 11:1, and say: **Let's take a look at what the Bible says about faith in Hebrews 11:1: "Now faith is being sure of what we hope for and certain of what we do not see."**

Even though we couldn't see inside the husk, we had faith that corn was in there! Even though we can't see God, we can have faith that he's there for us. The Bible tells us, other Christians tell us, and God tells us when we worship him and pray to him.

Say a prayer: **Thank you, God, for being there for us even though we can't see you. Help our faith to grow, just like the stalks of corn grow. In Jesus' name, amen.**

Give each of the children some candy corn. Say: **When you eat your candy corn, remember this message and always have faith!**

How Many Times?

Topic: Forgiveness

Scripture: Matthew 18:21-22

Simple Supplies: You'll need a Bible.

Ask:
- **When do we have to forgive people?**
- **Why does Jesus want us to forgive?**

Say: **There are a lot of times we need to forgive others. For example, maybe your brother or sister does something mean to you. Lots of times it's hard to forgive.**

Jesus had a lot to say about forgiveness. Open your Bible to Matthew 18:21-22. **Peter asked Jesus how many times we should**

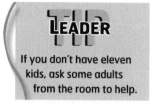

LEADER

If you don't have eleven kids, ask some adults from the room to help.

forgive someone—seven times? Jesus answered, "I tell you, not seven times, but seventy-seven times." Let's see what this looks like!

Ask one child to stand and hold up seven fingers. Say: **Peter asked Jesus if we should forgive someone seven times.** Then ask ten other children to join the first child and stand, each of them holding up seven fingers—a total of seventy-seven.

Jesus answered Peter, "Not seven times, but seventy-seven times." That's a lot of forgiving! So the next time someone is mean to you, think about how many times seventy-seven is, and ask Jesus to help you forgive!

Have the children sit down. Ask all the children to hold up seven fingers and join you in prayer. Say a line and have kids repeat after you. **Dear God** (pause)**, forgive us when we are mean to others** (pause)**, and help us to forgive others** (pause) **when they are mean to us** (pause)**. In Jesus' name, amen.**

Heavenly Help

Topic: Angels

Scripture: Matthew 18:10

Simple Supplies: You'll need a Bible, a tray, a first-aid kit, a toy horn or microphone, and an envelope with a sheet of paper inside. Place the first-aid kit, horn, and envelope on the tray.

Bring out the tray, and show the kids. Say: **I love to think about angels, don't you? The Bible tells us the many ways angels serve God and help us.** As you hold up each item from the tray one at a time, ask:

• **How do you think an angel would use this to serve God?**

Hold up the first-aid kit, and say: **Sometimes angels help people, like when they ministered to Jesus in the desert after he was tempted and in the garden right before he died.**

Hold up the envelope and take out the letter. Say: **Sometimes angels give messages to people, like when the angel told Mary she was going to have God's Son!**

Blow into the toy horn. Say: **Sometimes angels get people's attention with huge announcements, like when lots of angels filled the sky and told the shepherds that God's Son was born! Wow! I wish I could've seen that!**

Open your Bible to Matthew 18:10, and read: **"See that you do not look down on one of these little ones. For I tell you that their angels in heaven always see the face of my Father in heaven."**

Jesus said that angels watch over us, and they see God's face in heaven. Ask:

• **How do you feel knowing that angels take care of us?**
• **How can you thank God for making the angels?**

Say: **I feel great and special knowing that angels take care of us. Let's thank God for making angels.**

Choose a child to stand and hold up the first-aid kit, and pray: **Thank you, God, for letting the angels help Jesus when he was in the desert and right before he died.**

Choose another child to stand and hold up the envelope, and pray: **Thanks for the angel who told Mary the wonderful news that she was going to be Jesus' mother.**

Choose another child to stand and hold up the toy horn, and pray: **Thanks for all the angels who told the good news that Jesus was born.**

Then ask everyone to give one big group hug. **Thanks for the angels who watch over us. In Jesus' name, amen.**

That's a Long Time!

Topic: Eternal Life

Scripture: John 3:16

Simple Supplies: You'll need a Bible, a shoestring, and a skein of yarn.

Ask two children to stand up and each hold an end of a shoestring. Say: **Look at the length of this shoestring. It has a beginning and an end.** Then make an exaggerated show of unraveling the skein of yarn. **This bunch of yarn is lots longer than the shoestring, isn't it?** When it's unraveled as much as possible, let the others stand up and hold onto a part of it.

Open your Bible to John 3:16, and say: **The Bible tells us "For God so loved the world that he gave his one and only Son, that whoever believes in him shall not perish but have eternal life." That means we won't** *die* **forever, we'll** *live* **forever in heaven with Jesus!**

Our life on earth is like this shoestring. It is short with a beginning and an end.

Eternal life is even longer than the yarn. The yarn is longer than the shoestring, but even it has a beginning and an end. Eternal life is forever—no end. Ask:

- **What do you think eternal life in heaven will be like?**
- **Who can you tell about Jesus?**

Say: **I think eternal life will be like one big, happy family reunion and party. We'll get to be next to Jesus and sing praises to him. We'll be so happy. Let's tell everyone about Jesus so all of our loved ones will live forever with him in heaven.**

Ask everyone to hold onto the yarn, and pray: **Dear God, thanks for giving us Jesus so we can live forever. Help us tell everyone the good news. In Jesus' name, amen.**

Fears Dissolve

Topic: Facing Fears

Scripture: Isaiah 41:13

Simple Supplies: You'll need a Bible, a spoonful of salt, and a clear pitcher of water. Set the supplies on top of a table.

Ask:

• **What are some things you're afraid of?**

Say: **There are lots of things we can be afraid of. We might be afraid of a bully who lives down the street, or we might be afraid of losing our favorite pet.** Name other things kids mentioned. **Listen to what the Bible says about fear.**

Open your Bible to Isaiah 41:13, and read: **"For I am the Lord, your God, who takes hold of your right hand and says to you, Do not fear; I will help you."**

Hold up the spoonful of salt, and say: **Let's pretend this salt represents our fears. In a minute, I'll have you call out some of the things you said you were afraid of. When you call out your fears, pretend you're giving them to God. I'll show you what God does to your fears.**

Ask everyone to face a partner and hold each other's right hands. Say: **Imagine God is holding your right hand, like it says in our Bible verse. Now go ahead and tell me your fears.** As kids say their fears, pour the salt slowly into the pitcher of water. Then stir the water so the salt dissolves. Ask:

• **What happened to the salt?**
• **How did it feel telling God your fears and having someone hold your right hand?**

Say: **When we tell God our fears, he makes them dissolve. God gives us comfort and peace. The Bible tells us that God holds our right hand and not to be afraid. Let's tell everyone about our awesome God who loves us and tells us not to be afraid.**

Pray: **Dear God, it is so wonderful that you care so much for me and that you help me not be afraid. Help me tell others how wonderful you are. In Jesus' name, amen.**

What a Lift

Topic: Joy

Scripture: Nehemiah 8:10b

Simple Supplies: You'll need a Bible, an air-inflated balloon, and a helium-inflated balloon with a long string attached.

Say: **I'm wondering if there's a difference between *happiness* and *joy*. What do you think?** Let children respond, then bring out the balloons. **Let's pretend that this balloon** (hold up the air-filled one) **is happiness that comes from good things on earth. Let's pretend that this balloon** (hold up the helium-filled one) **is joy that comes from God. First, let's talk about happiness that comes from good things on earth.** Ask:

- **What things make you happy?**

Each time a child mentions something, have that child bop the balloon into the air. Kids might mention toys, chocolate, good grades, and so on. When they finish saying things, let the balloon float to the ground. Say: **Those are a lot of good things that make us happy. But happiness comes and goes just like this balloon that goes up and down.**

Hold up the helium-filled balloon. Ask:

- **What brings us joy from God?**

As kids mention things like obeying God, listening to parents, serving others, treating others kindly, or telling others about Jesus, hand the balloon to that child, letting the balloon float a little higher each time, until you're holding the end of the string. Then let it go!

Say: **Wow! The joy we get from God lifts us up. It's a joy that lasts.** Open your Bible to Nehemiah 8:10b, and read: **The Bible tells us "Do not grieve, for the joy of the Lord is your strength." That means don't be sad. God's joy strengthens us.**

Close in prayer: **Dear God, help us to obey you and do other things that bring joy from you. We want the joy from you to strengthen us and keep us flying high. In Jesus' name, amen.**

Cheering Up

Topic: Kindness

Scripture: Proverbs 12:25

Simple Supplies: You'll need a Bible.

Open your Bible to Proverbs 12:25, and say: **The Bible tells us that "an anxious heart weighs a man down, but a kind word cheers him up." I want to see what this looks like. OK?** Have the kids stand up, then ask:

- **What makes you anxious or worried?** With each thing kids say, have them slump down, down, and down, until they are lying on the floor. They might be worried they'll do poorly in school, worried they'll not make new friends, or worried about a parent's or grandparent's health, and so on.

Say: **Man, all those worries kinda weighed you down to the ground! What a heavy load! The Bible says that an anxious or worried heart weighs a person down!** Ask:

- **What are kind words you could use to cheer up people?** With each of the kind words, have kids stand up, up, and up. They might say, "It'll be OK," "Don't worry," "I'm your friend," and so on.

Say: **Those kind words cheered you up and lifted you off the ground. And that's just what the Bible says—kind words cheer** people up. The next time you're worried, pray or tell a friend about it. You'll feel better. The next time you see someone else who's worried, tell that person a kind, comforting word.

Close in prayer: **Dear God, we want to give all our worries to you. Thank you for all the people who are kind and loving in our lives. And thanks so much for the greatest kindness of all—Jesus! In his name, amen.**

Have kids go back to their seats and share a kind word or two with their families.

Give It Away

Topic: Service

Scripture: Luke 22:27b

Simple Supplies: You'll need a Bible and a bag of treats.

Say: **Welcome everyone. Before I start this lesson, I have one rule for you. You can't move. Let me see you sit as still as possible.** Pause. **Remember, you can't move until I tell you to do so.**

Bring out a bag of treats, and place it out of the children's reach. Move around animatedly as you talk: **Hmm. Here's this bag of treats, but you can't move to get it. What if I built a machine that would pick up the candy and drop it in your mouths? No, that wouldn't work. We don't have enough time for me to build something.**

I know! What if I train some ants to carry the candy to you? No, that won't work. I don't know where I'd find so many ants, and I don't have a clue how to train them.

You could add a few more zany ideas, but by now kids will probably say, "You give it to us!" **Oh yeah, I could give the treats to you!** Walk over to the treats, and hand them out to the children. Let the children move now! Ask:

- What was it like for you to wait for the treat?
- How did you feel when I finally gave it to you?
- How is this like us reaching out to others?

Say: **People are all around us who might not be able to help themselves. Maybe they're out of work or maybe they're hurt. We need to notice these people and reach out to them. Let's look out for people in our families, in our church, in our community, and in our world who need our help. Let's reach out to them by giving money, canned goods, or clothing, or maybe just kind and encouraging words.**

Open your Bible to Luke 22:27b, and say: **Jesus is our example in all we do. These are Jesus' own words: "I am among you as one who serves."**

Close by praying: **Dear Jesus, thank you for coming to earth to serve. Help us be like you. Help us notice people who need our help and reach out to them. We do this all in your holy name, amen.**

LEADER TIP

Use this message to kick off an outreach project, such as a clothing drive or canned food drive. Encourage kids to join in and reach out to those who need our help.

Help!

Topic: Sharing Faith

Scripture: 1 Timothy 2:3-4

Simple Supplies: You'll need a Bible and a life ring.

Open your Bible to 1 Timothy 2:3-4, and read it to the kids. Say: **Jesus wants all people to be saved and to know his truth.** Bring out the life ring. **Let's pretend that this life ring is our faith. This life ring is all we know about Jesus.**

Hand the life ring to a volunteer, then step away several feet. Ask:

- **In real life, if someone was swimming** (pretend to swim)**, and all of a sudden the person needed help** (wave your hands overhead)**, what would you do?** Wait for the volunteer to toss you the life ring.
- **What would happen if you kept that life ring to yourself?**

Hold onto the life ring, and say: **In real life, if someone needed our help in water, we'd throw the person a life ring! We wouldn't keep it to ourselves. But remember when I said let's pretend this life ring is our faith—all we know about Jesus?** Ask:

- **What if we hold onto our faith and not tell others about Jesus?**
- **Why should we share our faith?**
- **Who can you tell about Jesus today?**

Say: **Jesus wants everyone to be saved. All people need to know about how much Jesus loves them. Share your faith. Help the people who need to know about Jesus.**

Ask everyone to gather around the life ring as you pray: **Dear God, thank you for saving us through Jesus. Help us share our faith so others will know about Jesus too. In Jesus' name, amen.**

Jesus' Warm Love

Topic: Jesus' Love

Scripture: John 3:16

Simple Supplies: You'll need a Bible, a tub of cold water, and warm towels. If you're meeting inside, lay a tarp on the floor, and put the tub of cold water on it.

Read John 3:16 aloud to the children, then say: **Let's try an experiment before we talk about God's awesome love for us.**

Gather kids around the tub of cold water, and invite them to put their hands in it. Pause for a time for the children's hands to get cold. Ask:

- **What's it like having your hands in cold water?**

Hand out the towels, and invite the kids to dry off and warm up. Ask:

- **What's it like getting dry with a warm towel?**

Say: **Our hands were so cold, but then they got dry and warm with the towels. Oh, they feel so much better!** Invite the kids to keep their hands warm in the towels. Ask:

- **How is a warm towel like Jesus' love?**

Say: **Jesus loves us so much. With Jesus inside, we feel warm and comforted. Jesus loves us so much, he wants to live with us forever in heaven. Let's tell all people about Jesus who loves them.**

Encourage the children to hold onto the towels as you close in prayer: **Thank you, God, for your awesome love. Thanks for sending Jesus to help us feel warm and comforted, and so that we can live with you forever. In his name we pray, amen.**

LEADER

Make the water as cold as possible by placing ice cubes in it. Make the towels as warm as possible by putting them in a dryer close to the message time.

Jesus Forgives Us

Topics: Sin, Forgiveness

Scripture: Ephesians 1:7

Simple Supplies: You'll need a Bible, a robe, a permanent marker, a dry erase marker, eraser, paper towels with polish remover on them, and a white board. Invite another person to be Jesus and help during the message. Give your volunteer the robe to wear.

Gather the children, and read aloud Ephesians 1:7. Say: **The Bible tells us that through Jesus' blood, we have forgiveness of sins. Let's start out by you telling me some sins.** Ask:

- **What are bad things people do?** For each sin a child says, use the permanent marker to draw an X on the board.

Say: **OK. That's quite a bit of sins, wouldn't you say?** Use the eraser to try to erase them. They won't come off the board. Look terrified, like you've done something wrong.

Say: **I guess I should have used the other kind of marker! I think I need some help!**

Ask a volunteer to come up and use the dry erase marker to draw a heart shape over each X, covering it as completely as possible.

Look! Our sins are being covered. Remember our Bible verse that said through Jesus' blood, we have forgiveness of sins! "Jesus" nods and smiles, then erases each X with the paper towels.

Ask the children to close their eyes for a prayer. The volunteer can exit. Pray: **Dear Jesus, thank you for your life, death, and resurrection. Thanks that through you, our sins are forgiven. We love you, Lord. In Jesus' name, amen.**

Look at That

Topic: Seeing Jesus

Scripture: 1 Corinthians 13:12

Simple Supplies: You'll need a Bible, an aluminum pan lid, a sheet of aluminum foil, an aluminum pie plate, and a mirror.

Show kids the variety of things that reflect (but don't show the mirror yet). One at a time, have them look into the pan lid, aluminum foil, and pie plate. Ask:

- **How well can you see yourself in this?**

Say: **We couldn't see very well at all in these items.**

Open your Bible to 1 Corinthians 13:12, and read it to the kids. Then say: **The Bible says that right now we see the Lord dimly. Kind of like these reflections from the lid, aluminum foil, and pie plate. We know Jesus and love him, but we still live on earth. When we get to** *heaven*, **we'll see Jesus face to face. We'll see him and know him clearly, just like he sees us and knows us clearly right now.** Hold up the mirror so kids can see their clear reflections. Ask:

- **What do you think heaven will be like?**
- **What do you think you'll do when you see Jesus face to face?**

Say: **Heaven will be so awesome. All the people I love who love Jesus will be there. When I see Jesus, I want to thank him face to face for all he's done for me. Let's thank Jesus right now in a prayer.**

Pass the mirror, and have kids each look into it and say, "Dear Jesus, I want to see you face to face." Close by praying: **Thank you for dying for us so we can live forever with you in heaven. In Jesus' name, amen.**

Money, Money, Money

Topic: Offering

Scripture: Deuteronomy 15:7-8

Simple Supplies: You'll need a Bible, play money, and markers.

Give each child some play money. Ask the children to hold onto their money as you read Deuteronomy 15:7-8: **"If there is a poor man among your brothers in any of the towns of the land that the Lord your God is giving you, do not be hardhearted or tightfisted toward your poor brother. Rather be openhanded and freely lend him whatever he needs."** Ask:

- **What does it mean to be "tightfisted"?**

Say: **Let's see what it means to be tightfisted.** Ask the children to stand in a circle and hold the play money close to their chests. **When we're tightfisted, we want to keep all of our money to ourselves.**

Then ask kids to reach out, as if they're giving their money away to the children across the circle from them. **God wants us to be open-handed and freely give money to those who need it.** Ask:

- **Who are poor people we can give to?**
- **Why does God want us to give freely?**

Say: **When we give our money in church, it goes lots of places, like to missionaries in** [share some of your church's mission outreach programs]. **God wants us to give our money freely, because he's the one who's given us all of our blessings in the first place. When we give to others, we show God's love to others and we show God how much we trust him.**

Let the kids use the markers to draw crosses on their play money. Ask them to keep the play money where they can see it at home to remind them to always give freely.

Ask kids to hold their play money close, and pray: **Dear God, please help us not be tightfisted.** Ask kids to reach out with their play money. **Help us always be openhanded and give to the poor. Thank you for blessing us so much. In Jesus' name, amen.**

Family Reunion!

Topic: God's Children

Scripture: 1 John 3:1a

Simple Supplies: You'll need a Bible, cupcakes, and napkins. Bring enough cupcakes for each child to have one.

Ask:

- **Who created families?**
- **What does your family look like?**

Say: **God created families, and they all look different! Some have a mom and a dad, some have one parent, some have grandparents, some have guardians, some have lots of brothers and sisters, some have one brother or one sister, some have children who are born into the family, some have children who were adopted into the family.** Take a deep breath.

But you know what? Although families might look different, they're the same in one way: God created families to love and care for each other.

Open your Bible to 1 John 3:1a, and read: **"How great is the love the Father has lavished on us, that we should be called children of God!"** Ask:

- **What does the Bible verse mean?**

Say: **We're all God's children! We're all one big family of God! This calls for a celebration! I want a family reunion! You're all my brothers and sisters, and we're all children of God!** Bring out the cupcakes, and sing a praise song.

Close with prayer: **Thank you, God, for our families, no matter what they look like. But most of all, thank you for making us a part of the family of God. Now we all have lots of brothers and sisters, and it is a reason to celebrate. Thanks for sending Jesus who made all this possible. In his name, amen.**

LEADER

Host an even bigger family reunion by supplying cupcakes for the entire congregation. Have the children hand them out. Celebrate everyone being a child in God's big family!

Kettle of Kindness

Topic: Kindness

Scripture: 2 Samuel 9:1-13

Simple Supplies: You'll need a Bible, a big kettle, a large bag of popped corn, a measuring cup, a spoon, cups, and napkins.

Open your Bible to 2 Samuel 9:1-13, and say: **The Bible tells us that when David became king, he wanted to show kindness to a man named Mephibosheth. What a fun name! Everybody say it.** Mephibosheth! **Mephibosheth's dad, Jonathan, had been David's best friend. When his dad died, Mephibosheth lost his land as well as his father. Mephibosheth was afraid of the new king, David, because he didn't know him very well.**

Show kids your supplies. **While I tell you how King David was kind, we're going to make a kettle of kindness with some popcorn. Well, King David was kind to Mephibosheth and told him not to be afraid.** Pour a cup of popcorn into the kettle. **King David was kind, too, because he gave Mephibosheth land,** (pour in a cup of popcorn) **food,** (pour in another cup of popcorn) **and people to take care of him.** Stir the kettle of popcorn. **Wow! What a bunch of kind things to do.** Ask:

• **How can we treat others kindly?**

For each idea kids mention, let them take turns pouring in more popcorn and stirring the pot. Say: **We can be kind to others by helping them, by saying nice words, and by telling them how much Jesus loves them. After we say a prayer, I have another way we can be kind to each other.**

Close in prayer: **Dear God, we want to treat others with kindness, just as David treated Mephibosheth. Help us remember how kind and loving you were in sending Jesus to us. In his name, amen.**

Have the kids be kind and serve each other cups of popcorn.

A "Hope" Transplant

Topic: Hope

Scripture: Psalms 39:7; 42:5-6a; 71:5; 119:147

Simple Supplies: You'll need a Bible, a table, an old sheet, a doctor's coat, tongs, slips of paper, pen, and scissors.

Write the Scripture references on slips of paper, and place them in your Bible. Write each of the following words on a separate slip of paper: "doubt," "anxiety," "fear," and "unbelief." Before the message, ask a volunteer to be your patient. Have the volunteer lie on the table. Lay the slips of paper with the negative words on the volunteer's chest. Cover the person with a sheet. Put on the doctor's coat.

Invite the children forward, and say: **Welcome, ladies and gentlemen! Our "patient" here is in desperate need of a transplant! Some "nasty" items are weighing our patient down. They must be removed. First I'll have to make an incision.**

Cut a slit in the sheet in the area of the chest. Pick up the tongs, pull out the "doubt" slip of paper, and hold the slip high.

Say: **Ah! Here's one of the problems! "Doubt!" What a heavy problem this is! People who are full of doubt mistrust everyone and are uncertain of their future. We must get rid of this fellow.**

Drop the slip of paper to the floor.

Say: **Let's see what else is causing problems. OK! I see another item that needs to be removed!**

Fish around with the tongs, and pull out the slip that says "anxiety."

Say: **Ew! "Anxiety!" This one causes trouble in the mind! It makes people uncertain and full of fear about the future! And speaking of fear...**

Pull out the "fear" slip.

Say: **I might as well get rid of that, too! This poor, poor patient! I'm beginning to see a pattern here! With all these heavy, negative things inside, our patient can't have much hope. We all need to have hope. Let me just check here, oh yes, I see one more thing I need to remove before I do the transplant.**

Pull out the "unbelief" slip.

Say: **"Unbelief!" If we have nothing good or no one to believe in, it's no wonder those other problems can begin to grow. Now that I have those bad things removed, we can replace them with something good.**

Open your Bible, and read Psalm 39:7. **Hope in the Lord! Now that's something to look forward to. I will just transplant that into our patient.**

Tuck the paper in through the slit with the tongs. Read Psalm 42:5-6a.

Say: **Now this is a good one to put in the spot where fear used to grow. We don't need to be afraid when our hope is in God.**

Tuck it in. Then read Psalm 71:5.

Say: **Yes! This will work! Confidence in our Lord! The person who wrote this Bible verse said he had hope in God since he was a young person.**

Tuck it in through the slit with the tongs, then look at the patient's face.

Say: **Oh, I can just see the color coming back into my patient's cheeks already!**

Read Psalm 119:147.

Say: **There, now this verse tells us there's hope in God's Word— the Bible. This will help our patient know that when doubts or fears creep in, he [she] can turn to God's Word and find strength.**

I think this surgery has been a total success, and I expect a full recovery for my patient!

Assist the patient off the table, then give the volunteer a round of applause.

LEADER

It would be funny to have someone else "wheel" your patient out of the room into Recovery. Do you have a wheelchair anywhere you could use?

Ask:

- **When do you suffer from some of the same problems our patient had?**
- **How can you remember to have hope?**

Say: **We all suffer from doubt, anxiety, fear, and unbelief at times. But we need to remember to listen to God's Word and have hope that God is in control of our lives. We can always have hope and trust that God loves us.**

Close with prayer: **Dear God, it is so easy to let fear, worry, and doubt creep into my heart and push the hope and joy out.**

Help me remember that your Word is where the truth is. In Jesus' name, amen.

When Life Gives You a Lemon

Topic: Good Will Come

Scripture: Deuteronomy 31:8

Simple Supplies: You'll need a Bible, small slices of lemon, and a bag of lemon drop candies or cups of sweet lemonade.

Ask:

- **Have you ever heard the saying "When life gives you lemons, make lemonade"?**
- **What do you suppose that means?**

Say: **It means that when bad things happen, try to make good things come from it.** Let any volunteers taste a tiny bit of lemon. Ask:

- **What's the lemon taste like?**
- **What are some bad things that happen in life?**

Say: **My lemon slice tasted sour. Sometimes bad things happen that seem sour. Like death and divorce.** Name other things the children mentioned. **No matter what happens in life, we need to remember that God is in control.**

Open your Bible to Deuteronomy 31:8, and read it to the children. Say: **God also promises never to leave us. When we turn our difficult situation over to God, it's sort of like taking the lemon and making lemonade.**

Pass out the lemon candy or cups of lemonade. Say: **We may not like our circumstances, but by asking God to add a little "sugar"** to the situation and to help us, we'll be making the best we can out of something bitter.

As kids enjoy the sweet treat, pray: **Dear God, we give you anything that's troubling us.** Pause for kids to silently pray. **We trust you to help us handle our problems. Thanks for friends and family who comfort us too. In Jesus' name, amen.**

The Judge

Topic: Criticism

Scripture: Matthew 7:1-2; John 8:3-11

Simple Supplies: You'll need a Bible, a choir robe, a gavel or hammer, a table, a chair, and two sheets of poster board—one that says in big letters "Criticism" and another that says "Love." Put on the choir robe before the message begins.

Display the two signs so everyone can see them. After you enter and sit down, rap the gavel on the table. Say: **Hear ye! Hear ye! This court is now in session. I'm here today to consider the case of Criticism vs. Love.** Motion to each sign as you say the words. Ask:

• **Who can tell me what it means to criticize someone?**

Say: **It means to find fault with or to judge unfairly. Let me give you an example from my book of law.** Hold up your Bible, then open it to John 8:3-11.

The Pharisees were a group of religious leaders. They made a woman stand before Jesus to be judged. The Pharisees knew the woman had done something wrong, but instead of helping her change by being kind to her, they criticized her. They said, "Jesus, this woman is bad, you must punish her. It's the law, you have to punish her!"

Jesus said that if anyone of them had never done anything wrong, then that person could punish her. Ask:

- **Who here has never done anything wrong?**

Say: **We've all done bad things. The problem with criticizing others is that we aren't perfect either. The Pharisees knew they'd all done bad things, so they left the woman alone. Jesus forgave her because Jesus is love.**

Turn in your Bible to Matthew 7:1-2. Say: **Referring back to my law book, Jesus says we are not to judge others or else we will be judged also. We need to follow Jesus' example and show love to others rather than criticize them. In the case of Criticism vs. Love, I find that love is the clear winner every time!** Bang the gavel on the table. **Case dismissed!**

Close in a prayer. Have kids raise their right hands and repeat after you:

Dear God,
Help us not criticize.
Help us show love.
In Jesus' name, amen.

What Happens When

Topic: Consequences

Scripture: Philippians 4:13

Simple Supplies: You'll need a Bible and a bag filled with these items: a flashlight, a hammer, an instrument such as a harmonica, and a plastic spider or snake.

Bring out the bag, and say: **Let's play a game called "What Happens When." I'll show you an item and then ask you what the result is when I use the item.** Ask:

- **If I'm in a dark room, what happens when I turn this on?** Take out the flashlight and flip the switch. **The result is light!**

- **What happens when I blow on this?** Take out the instrument and blow. **The result is noise!**
- **What happens when I hit a nail with this?** Take out the hammer, and act like you'll hammer a nail. **A nail would be hammered into a board. If I hit my thumb, there would be a different result!**
- **What happens when you see this?** Take out the plastic spider or snake, and wait for kids' reactions such as screams or laughter!

Say: **Everything we do has a result or a consequence. Like if we follow rules or don't follow rules.** Ask:

- **What rules do you have at home?**
- **What happens when you follow the rules?**
- **What happens when you don't follow the rules?**

Say: **Everything we do or don't do has a consequence. When we don't follow the rules, work doesn't get done and people's feelings might get hurt. When we do follow the rules, life is more peaceful and we get along better.**

Open your Bible to Philippians 4:13, and say: **The Bible tells us that we can do everything through Jesus who gives us strength. When you need help to do the right thing, ask Jesus for help. He'll give you strength.**

Choose children to come up and hold the items you used. Ask each child holding an item to pray for Jesus to help him or her to do the right things, but give children the option of not praying aloud. Close in prayer: **Dear God, thank you for sending Jesus. It is so wonderful to know that he is there to help us with everything we need. In his name, amen.**

Helping Friends

Topic: Friendship

Scripture: Philippians 2:1-3

Simple Supplies: You'll need a Bible.

Form partners, and have them stand back to back. Say: **Hook arms with your partner, and try to sit down then stand back up. Help each other do this amazing feat!** Pause while partners sit down, then stand back up.

Once everyone tries that partner activity, ask them to stand face to face, about a foot apart. Say: **Try it again. Only this time, hold your partner's hands, try to sit down, and stand back up. Help each other do this!** Ask:

- **How did you help each other sit down then stand back up?**
- **How is this like friends helping each other every day?**

Say: **You were aware of your partner and how he or she was standing or sitting. You worked together to sit down and stand back up. You also had fun doing it. Friends have fun together.**

Open your Bible to Philippians 2:1-3, and show kids the words. Say: **The Bible tells us that friends help, encourage, and comfort each other. When friends need help, we help them.**

Ask all the partners to help each other stand, then join hands. Pray: **Dear God, thanks for all the friends in this room you've blessed us with. In Jesus' name, amen.**

Healthful Choices

Topic: Health

Scripture: 1 Corinthians 6:19

Simple Supplies: You'll need a Bible and a pet (for example, bring in a puppy on a leash or a cat in a pet carrier).

Say: **Look what I brought to show you! My pet! I love my pet, and I'm so glad God gave it to me to take care of.** Ask:
- **How do you think I take care of my pet?**
- **Why should I treat my pet with care?**

Say: **I feed my pet good food and fresh water. I brush my pet and take it on walks. I keep my pet healthy by doing all these things. I do it because I love my pet!** Ask:
- **How do you take care of yourself?**
- **Why does God want you to take care of yourself?**

Say: **We take care of ourselves when we eat good food, drink lots of water, keep ourselves clean, and get exercise. We take care of our bodies because God loves us and wants us to be healthy.**

Open your Bible to 1 Corinthians 6:19, and read it to the children.

Say: **Wow! The Bible says the Holy Spirit lives in us, and we need to honor God with our bodies. That's the best reason of all to take care of ourselves.**

Close in prayer: **Dear God, thank you that you care about all of us, even our bodies. Help us to make good healthy choices about how to take care of ourselves. In Jesus' name, amen.**

Let the kids say goodbye to your pet.

Jesus Died

Topic: Bullies

Scripture: Matthew 27:28-30

Simple Supplies: You'll need a Bible and a dark trash bag with small, inexpensive toys inside (enough for each child).

Bring out the trash bag, and open your Bible to Matthew 27:28-30. Say: **Today we're going to talk about Jesus' death. It's a sad story, but it has a happy ending. When you look at this trash bag, you might think, "Nothing good ever comes out of trash bags," but trust me, something good will come!**

The Bible tells us that Jesus was hurt by mean people before he died. People made fun of him, hit him, and then put him on a cross to die. Ask:

- **How many of you have bullies in your school or neighborhood?**

Say: **Jesus had bullies in his time too. The amazing thing about Jesus is that he asked God to forgive the mean people because they didn't understand what they were doing.** Ask:

- **If Jesus could forgive the mean people before he died, can we forgive bullies?**

Say: **Jesus helps us forgive people who hurt us. Jesus loves bullies because Jesus loves the whole world! He's sad when bullies are mean. But if they say they're sorry, Jesus will forgive them, and he wants us to forgive them too.**

Open up the trash bag, and give kids the toys. Say: **I told you my story has a happy ending. Jesus didn't stay dead. He rose from the dead and lives forever in heaven. Jesus died for all people, and he wants all people to say they're sorry, receive forgiveness, then live forever with him.**

Pray: **Dear God, please forgive us when we're mean to others. Please help us forgive those who are mean to us. Thank you for dying on the cross and forgiving our sins. Thanks for eternal life with you. In Jesus' name, amen.**

God Is Always With You

Topic: Moving Away

Scripture: Deuteronomy 31:8

Simple Supplies: You'll need a Bible, a long strip of butcher paper, and crayons. Write out Deuteronomy 31:8 on the butcher paper.

Ask:

• **Who has ever moved to a new place?**
• **How did you feel when you moved?**

Say: **We may move to a new home, a new city, a new state, or even a new country. It can be fun, but it also can be scary. We might feel these same feelings if we move to a new school, too!**

Open your Bible to Deuteronomy 31:8, and read: **"The Lord himself goes before you and will be with you; he will never leave you nor forsake you. Do not be afraid; do not be discouraged."**

Have the kids each place one foot on the butcher paper and use crayons to trace around it. Encourage the kids who can write their names to do so on the paper as well. As kids do this, ask:

• **How does it make you feel knowing that God is with you wherever you go?**

Join hands around the butcher paper, then pray: **Thanks, God, that you are with us wherever we go. We never need to be afraid. In Jesus' name, amen.**

Ask kids to carry the banner so all can see, then post it near the church entrance. The sign will remind people that God is always with them wherever they go!

God Made People

Topic: Creation

Scripture: Genesis 1:26–2:25

Simple Supplies: You'll need a Bible and a box filled with blocks, plastic construction toys such as Legos, and a variety of sizes of balls.

Form groups of no more than four, and give each group some of the building supplies, then say: **Our story today is about when God made people. But first, I want you to have a hand in creating something. You have two minutes to work with your group to create a person out of the supplies. Ready? Create!**

Encourage kids as they work. Call time after two minutes, then ask:

- **How did you feel trying to create something from the supplies?**
- **How do you think God felt as he created people?**

Say: **You did an awesome job with your creations. You had fun working together too. I think God must have had some fun when he was creating people.**

Open your Bible to Genesis 1:31, and read: **"God saw all that he had made, and it was very good."**

Call the children's names, and have them stand up by their people creations. Say: [Name of child]**, God made you and he did a great job!** Continue until everyone is standing, then you stand as well, and have the kids say the affirmation for you! On the count of three say all together: "Thanks for making us, God."

Blessing Bubbles

Topic: Blessings

Scripture: Romans 10:12b

Simple Supplies: You'll need a Bible and bubble gum. Chew a piece of the gum before the message so it's ready for you to blow a bubble! Make sure you have enough bubble gum for each child.

> **LEADER TIP**
>
> The more pieces of gum you chew at the same time, the bigger the bubble! If time allows, give kids a quick "bubble-blowing" lesson.

Blow a bubble, then pop it. Say: **Many people learn to blow bubbles with gum when they're children. Every time I see a bubble, I think of happy times and the good times and blessings I had growing up.**

Open your Bible to Romans 10:12b. Say: **Listen to this! The Bible says, "The same Lord is Lord of all and richly blesses all who call on him." God richly blesses each one of us! I'll blow another bubble, and you all shout out blessings such as "family," "friends," "this church," and "Jesus." Let's see how many blessings we can name before my bubble pops.**

> **LEADER TIP**
>
> Gum can be a choking hazard for young children, so have stickers or an optional treat on hand if your group includes little ones.

Give each person a piece of bubble gum, then say: **Chew your gum, and tell God thanks for all your blessings.**

Close by praying: **Thank you God for everything you do for us, especially for sending Jesus. In his name, amen.**

Praise the Lord

Topic: Praise

Scripture: Psalm 150

Simple Supplies: You'll need a Bible and a variety of colors of construction paper.

As the children come forward, pass out different colored sheets of construction paper. Line up the children in front of the room.

Say: **The Bible tells us to praise the Lord always! So let's do it now. I'll read Psalm 150 to you. Each time you hear me say the word "praise," lift your sheet of construction paper high, then bring it back down. Ready?**

"Praise the Lord. Praise God in his sanctuary; praise him in his mighty heavens. Praise him for his acts of power; praise him for his surpassing greatness. Praise him with the sounding of the trumpet, praise him with the harp and lyre, praise him with tambourine and dancing, praise him with the strings and flute, praise him with the clash of cymbals, praise him with resounding cymbals. Let everything that has breath praise the Lord. Praise the Lord."

Everyone take a deep breath! Good job! Ask:

- **Why do you want to praise God?**
- **Why do you think God is so good to us?**

Say: **I want to praise God because I love him. God is so good to us because he loves us. God is love, so let's always praise him.**

Pray: **We *praise* you, God. In Jesus' name, amen.** Have kids lift their papers one last time!

Spread the News

Topic: Sharing Faith

Scripture: Matthew 4:23-25

Simple Supplies: You'll need a Bible and a party popper.

LEADER TIP

Purchase party poppers at a craft store or a discount store. They contain confetti and streamers inside. For easy cleanup, lay a blanket or plastic tarp on the floor.

Hold up the party popper, then say: **We use party poppers when we have something to celebrate. Watch this!** Pull the string and pop the popper so the colorful streamers and confetti spreads. **Wow! Look at how the confetti and streamers spread on the floor!**

Open your Bible to Matthew 4:23-25, and say: **The Bible tells about Jesus teaching, preaching, and healing. News of Jesus spread all over the place, because everyone was in awe of his power!** Ask:

- **What news should we spread about Jesus?**
- **Why should we tell others about Jesus?**

Say: **We have the most joyful news to spread to everyone. Jesus loves you and wants to live with you forever. Spread the news!**

Close in prayer: **Jesus, I love you so much. Help me to spread the celebration news to everyone I meet. In your name, amen.**

Encourage kids to go back to their seats and spread the good news. Have them tell at least two others: "Jesus loves you, spread the news."

Messages for Holiday Stories

Apples of His Eye

Topic: New Year's Day

Scripture: 2 Corinthians 5:17

Simple Supplies: You'll need a Bible, party hats, apples, apple slicer or knife, caramel dip, paper plates, and napkins. The night before you give the message, cut up an apple, and set it out so it browns and shrivels. (Red Delicious apples work best.)

As the children come up for the message, pass out party hats. Say: **Happy new year, everybody! We're going to have our very own New Year's party right here and right now! We've got the party hats! We even have party food! We're going to have some delicious apple slices with caramel dip—yum!** Bring out a plate of brown apple slices that have sat out overnight in the open air. **Here we go! Our delicious apples! How do they look?** Show them to the children, and allow them to respond. **You know, our apples do look a little...well, yucky. They're kind of brown and shriveled—not exactly what we were expecting, right?**

Well, let's think for a minute about what our party food was for. We're celebrating the new year, right? That means we have a clean slate, a whole brand-new year to do better at all the things we didn't do such a great job at last year! For example, maybe some of you didn't do that great at being nice to your brother or sister. Tell the kids something you want to try to do better this new year. Ask:

• **What are some things you want to do better this new year?**

Say: **Maybe you want to try and pay better attention to your teachers at school.** Mention other things kids said. **Well, we get a whole new year to try and do better things. This is a clean slate!**

The Bible tells us about another clean slate we have. Let's see what it says. Open your Bible to 2 Corinthians 5:17, and read the verse aloud. **"Therefore, if anyone is in Christ, he is a new creation; the old has gone, the new has come!"** This means that when we ask for forgiveness, Jesus forgives us! Everything bad we've ever done is totally forgiven. We are new creations! And what better time to celebrate that we are new creations than with the new year?

Bring out fresh apples and an apple slicer. Show kids the fresh-looking apples. Let them dip in the caramel, and as they eat, pray: **God, I am so grateful that you will make me clean and new, just like this new year. Help me do a better job on the things in my life that please you. In Jesus' name, amen.**

God Loves Everyone

Topic: Martin Luther King Jr. Day

Scripture: John 4:1-26

Simple Supplies: You'll need a Bible.

Say: **This week we celebrate the birthday of a man who understood how our differences make us all special. Martin Luther King Jr. was a great man who helped people realize that we are all the same on the inside—it doesn't matter if we are black, white, tall, short, weak, or strong. Martin Luther King behaved a lot like Jesus in the way he treated people.**

Open your Bible to John 4:1-26, and show the children the words. Say: **The Bible tells about how some people treated others from a country named Samaria.** Have kids each find a partner and stand back to back. **It's kind of like how you are standing. They wanted nothing to do with Samaritans. They turned their backs on each other.**

But not Jesus. He treated all people with love. Jesus talked with a Samaritan woman. He told her that God loved her no matter who she was or what she had done, and she could live forever with him! She was so happy, she told other people from

Samaria. **Because of her, lots of people heard about our awesome God who loves everyone!** Have kids turn to face their partners and hug or give a high five. **That's how God wants us to treat everyone.** Ask:

• **Have you ever felt different from everyone else? When?**

Say: **What if God had made all of us the same? The same colors, the same talents, the same personalities? Pretty boring, huh?** Have kids stand back to back with their partners again. **We all have felt different at one time or another. Maybe it was in a good way—like you were the only one who got an A+ on the big math test, or maybe you're the only one in your family who can play a musical instrument. But maybe you've felt different before because of something not so great. Like maybe you were the "new kid" or maybe all your friends have brand-new bikes while you're stuck riding your older brother's hand-me-down bike.**

Sometimes people can be mean to people who are different from them. But God wants us to treat everyone with love—just as Jesus did. Have kids hug their partners or give high fives.

Close in prayer: **Thank you, God, for sending people like Martin Luther King who help us see people the way you see them. Help us every day to thank you for our differences and treat others with the love of Jesus. In his name, amen.**

Seasonal Shadows

Topic: Groundhog Day

Scripture: Ecclesiastes 3:1

Simple Supplies: You'll need a Bible and a picture of a groundhog.

Hold up the picture of the groundhog, then ask kids if they know what it is. Say: **This is a groundhog. There's a fun tradition about groundhogs. Groundhogs are said to be able to predict when winter will be over.** Have the children each find a partner. Have one partner be a groundhog and the other one be the weather. Have all the groundhogs crouch down. **Tradition says that on the morning of February 2, the groundhog comes out of its hole.** Have the groundhogs pretend to cautiously climb out of their holes. **If it's cloudy, the groundhog thinks that winter will soon be over.** Have the other child in each pair hover over the groundhog.

But, if it's sunny, the groundhog's own shadow scares him and he goes back into his hole for six more weeks of winter. Have the "weather" child hold his or her arms and fingers spread out over the groundhog, and have the groundhog crouch back down on the floor.

This is a fun tradition, but in truth, only God knows the seasons and when the weather will begin to warm up for spring.

Open your Bible to Ecclesiastes 3:1. Say: **The Bible says that "there is a time for everything, and a season for every activity under heaven."**

On Groundhog Day, let's have fun with this tradition, and each time we see the cute little groundhog, let's remember who made Mr. Groundhog and all the seasons—God!

Close in prayer: **Thank you, God, for making groundhogs and for all the weather you send. We are so glad that you are in control of everything. In Jesus' name, amen.**

Earth Day, Hooray!

Topic: Earth Day

Scripture: Psalm 24:1

Simple Supplies: You'll need a Bible and two containers: one with dirt and a plant and one with dirt and litter (crumpled paper and a crushed can).

Say: **We celebrate Earth Day this week. Earth Day is when we take time to think about our world and how we take care of it. Let's see what God has to say about the earth.** Open your Bible to Psalm 24:1, and read: **"The earth is the Lord's, and everything in it, the world, and all who live in it."** Ask:

- **According to the verse, who does the earth belong to?**
- **How do you think we should take care of the earth?**

Say: **The earth belongs to God. Our job is to take care of it. But when we look around, sometimes we see that we have "broken" God's earth by not taking good care of it. Look what I have here.**

Ask for volunteers to hold up each container.

Say: **In this container I have a beautiful plant, and in this one I have some yucky trash. The plant reminds us of the incredible creations God made on the earth, and the other container reminds us of how badly we can mess it up.** Ask:

- **How can we treat God's creation well?**

Say: **Let's take care of God's creation. Let's plant trees, water them, and keep our water clean. Let's never litter! To help remind us of our verse today, let's play a quick game called "Scripture Pop-Up." You will be plants popping up out of the ground. First let's all crouch down really low. When I point to you, I want you to "pop up" and say the next word in our verse. Are you ready? Let's say the verse together three times first. "The earth is the Lord's, and everything in it!"** Say this three times with the children.

Great! Now remember, when I point to you, pop up and say the next word in the verse. Play until everyone has had a turn to pop up!

Close by thanking God: **Dear God, you are so amazing. You made this wonderful earth and everything in it. Help us to remember it belongs to you and so we need to care for it well. In Jesus' name, amen.**

Then say: **Here's a game for you to play at home. This week, whenever our verse "pops" into your mind—whenever you think of our verse—I want you to do one thing to help God's earth. You may pick up some trash, you may recycle something, or you may want to plant flowers or a tree. Whatever you do, remember that you're honoring God by taking care of something that's his!**

The Humble King

Topic: Palm Sunday

Scripture: Matthew 21:1-11

Simple Supplies: You'll need a Bible, coats, and palm branches.

Say: **Palm Sunday is when we remember Jesus going to Jerusalem before he would suffer and die for us.** Open your Bible to Matthew 21:1-11, and show the children the words.

The Bible says that crowds were ahead of Jesus and behind Jesus. They laid coats and palm branches on the road before him. The people did this to show honor to a king. People were expecting Jesus to be like an earthly king who would save them from the mean people who were ruling them at that time, the Romans! The people didn't understand that Jesus was our forever king, God's Son! Jesus was coming to pay for people's sins and to change people's hearts, not rule as an earthly king.

Jesus chose to ride into Jerusalem on a donkey. He was gentle and humble, and that is why he chose the donkey—an animal that represented peace and humility. Ask:

• **What does it mean to be humble?**

Say: **When you're humble, you don't want to put on a big show. Let's explore what that might look like. Suppose you were playing a sport, like soccer or hockey, and you ended up making the winning goal. Well, there are two ways you can act in that situation—you could either choose to be humble or you could choose to be proud. Show me what it looks like if you make the winning goal and you look proud.** Lead the kids in looking proud! **Being humble does not mean that you put yourself down. There's a big difference! When you're humble, you let your actions do the talking for you. You don't have to brag about the things you've done because your actions speak louder than anything you could ever say. Show me what you'd look like if you'd just made a winning goal but you were humble.** Lead kids in showing humility, like simply smiling and waving.

When Jesus came to Jerusalem, he didn't come in proud and bragging about all the things he'd done. He didn't try to make himself look important by riding in on a fancy horse. No, he chose to come in quietly and with a gentle strength.

Ask kids to form two lines facing each other. Have them line the "road" between them with the coats and palm branches. Ask kids to imagine Jesus is riding on the road on the donkey. Then have a praise prayer. Ask the kids to shout praises about what we know about who Jesus is. Say: **Jesus is God's Son. Jesus is the king! Because of Jesus, we'll live forever.** End by saying: **Thank you, God, for sending Jesus to us. Thank you that we will get to live in heaven forever because of what Jesus did. In his name, amen.**

Jesus Gave It All

Topic: Ash Wednesday

Scripture: Matthew 16:24-25

Simple Supplies: You'll need a Bible, a basket of stickers and prepackaged snacks such as snack cakes or candy bars, a sheet of butcher paper, tape, and markers. Tape the butcher paper to one wall, and set the markers close by.

Say: **Today we are talking about Ash Wednesday. This is the first Wednesday of the season called "Lent" which leads us to Easter.** Open your Bible to Matthew 16:24-25, and show the children the words. **Jesus told his disciples, "If anyone would come after me, he must deny himself and take up his cross and follow me." "Taking up our cross" means we follow Jesus' example, even though it's hard to do.** Ask:

- **How did Jesus treat people?**
- **How can we act the same way Jesus did?**

Say: **Jesus loves people. Jesus gave up his life so we could spend eternity with him. It's hard to give up something. During these next weeks, many Christians give up things they really like so they can show honor to Jesus and remember what he did for us on the cross.** Ask:

- **What can you give up this time before Easter?**
- **How does that help us focus on Jesus?**

Say: **Maybe you can give up watching your favorite TV show and during that time read the Bible. Or maybe you could give up drinking your favorite soda then give the money you would have spent to a needy family. Remember, when we give up something it helps us focus on Jesus who gave up his *life* for us.**

Give each child a sheet of stickers and a prepackaged snack. Explain to them not to eat the snacks. Then motion to the butcher paper on the wall.

Say: **This week we are going to practice giving up something. I'm going to encourage each of you to give up your snack and your stickers. And if you choose to do so, your snack will be given to a child just like you who comes to our local outreach center.** Add the name of a place in town that serves needy children. **We're going to place our stickers all over this giant sheet of paper and write special notes or draw pictures to give to the children. By giving up these things, we will definitely make someone's day a lot brighter by sharing God's love with them.**

Pause for children to decorate the butcher paper.

LEADER

If you are leading the children's message during a church service and need it to go quickly, have the children draw a simple design such as a smiley face, then stick on a few stickers. Encourage them to come back after the service to complete their drawing. Ask adults to add their designs as well!

Hold the empty basket, and gather the children around you. Encourage them to give up their snacks to honor Jesus. However, do not force children to do this. Set the basket on the floor, and have the children join hands in a circle around it. Lead the children in prayer: **Dear Jesus, you have done so much for us, it is hard to understand. Please take these small things we are willing to give up, and use them to bless others who don't have as much as we do. Help them to understand how much you love them. In your name, amen.** Set a time when everyone can deliver the snacks and sign.

The Good, the Bad, and the Hope of Friday

Topic: Good Friday

Scripture: Matthew 27:27-54

Simple Supplies: You'll need a Bible, two boxes, dirt, treats, wrapping paper, newspaper, and tape. Place the dirt in one box, and wrap it beautifully! Place the treats in the other box, and wrap it with torn newspaper.

ALLERGY ALERT

LEADER TIP

Exaggerate the difference even more by beautifully wrapping the largest box possible (with dirt inside) and wrapping the tiniest box possible (with treats inside) in dirty, torn newspaper.

Say: **Good news, gang! I've got a special gift for you all today! But I decided to let you pick which one you want. There is this lovely, beautifully wrapped gift.** Hold it up. **Or, there is this rather torn-up gift.** Hold it up. **Which one do you choose, show me by raising your hands. This one?** Hold up the beautifully wrapped gift. **Or this one?** Hold up the torn-up gift.

It looks like we get the present inside this beautiful box. It looks beautiful, so good things must be inside. Open the package, and let the kids see the dirt. Grab a handful, hold it high, and let it trickle through your fingers. Aw, just dirt! Well, look at this other box. It's torn up, not very pretty. Nothing good can be in here! Well, let's see. Open that box, and let the children see the treats.

Distribute the treats, then say: **Many times**

LEADER TIP

The children more than likely will choose the beautiful gift. If they vote for the torn-up one, go along with it. Say, "Let's see what we would've received if we would have chosen this beautiful gift. You made the right choice!"

in life, good things come out of situations that look like they might be bad situations. For instance, suppose you're told you're going to church camp for a week. You don't know any other kids who will be there, and you don't like camping. But you go, and by the end of the week, you walk away with a ton **of new friends and you can't wait to go back the next year!**

Open your Bible to Matthew 27, and show the kids the words. Say: **Today we are talking about Good Friday. Friday was the day that Jesus died on the cross. So why do we call it good? I'll tell you why! You see, Jesus took our sins with him and died on the cross. Because of that Friday, we know that our sins are forgiven. And best of all, because of that Friday, we get to spend forever with Jesus in heaven. Now isn't that a good Friday?**

Close in prayer by having kids say, "Thank you Jesus for dying for me. In Jesus' name, amen." Then pray: **Help us, Lord, to share the news about Good Friday to others who don't know what you did for them. In your name, amen.**

Encourage kids to enjoy their good snacks that came out of a little torn-up box.

 One leader was excitedly describing how the women found the empty tomb on Easter morning. "He's alive! He's risen!" the leader exclaimed. One little four-year-old was unimpressed. She raised her hand and asked, "Didn't Jesus do that last year?"

Seeing Is Believing

Topic: Easter

Scripture: John 20:19-31

Simple Supplies: You'll need a Bible, a live chick, and a shoe box. Go to a local feed store, and purchase or borrow a baby chick. Poke air holes in the lid of the shoe box. Right before the message time, place the chick inside the box.

Place the shoe box behind you, and open your Bible to John 20:19-31. Say: **Easter is a time when we remember that Jesus died on the cross for our sins and then rose from the grave. The Bible tells us that some of his followers believed Jesus was alive. But there** was one disciple who didn't believe what was happening. **Thomas said, "I will not believe Jesus is alive unless I can see him and touch the nail holes in his hands." We can be like Thomas too. We can sometimes doubt as well. Let's try a little doubt experiment.** Hold the shoe box on your lap, then ask:

- **Who believes I have a baby chick inside this box?** Pause for kids to raise hands.
- **Do you really believe?**

Say: **Well if you believe me, then you can go back to your seats and have a great day.** The kids won't move. **You want to see in the box! But if you believe me, you don't need to see inside!** Pause for kids' reactions. **Well, OK. Let's all be like Thomas and see before we believe!** Lift off the lid, and hold the baby chick. **I was telling the truth! I did have a chick in my box. God wants you to believe the truth. Jesus is alive. God wants us to believe in Jesus even though we can't see him.**

Say a prayer: **Dear God, thank you for Jesus. Thank you that he rose again on the third day. Help us when we have doubts like Thomas. We love you. In your name we pray, amen.** Hold the chick for the rest of the people to see while the kids go back to their seats.

Come and See

Topic: Easter

Scripture: Matthew 28:5-6

Simple Supplies: You'll need a Bible and an empty box with a lid. Glue a picture of an angel to the inside of the lid. Make a copy of the illustration on page 242 if you need a picture of an angel.

ALLERGY ALERT

Say: **Come and see what I have today! What do you expect to be in this box?** Let the children respond. If it's a shoe box, they'll expect shoes. Then open the box lid. Show them the empty box.

Permission to photocopy this picture from *The Humongous Book of Children's Messages* granted for local church use. Copyright © Group Publishing, Inc., P.O. Box 481, Loveland, CO 80539. www.grouppublishing.com

It's empty! That's not what you expected, is it? That's just what happened on the first Easter morning! Just like we were surprised to find the box empty, some of Jesus' friends were surprised to see Jesus' tomb empty. You see, Jesus had been killed, and his body was placed in a tomb.

Early on the third day, though, some of Jesus' friends came to take care of his body. But when they got to the tomb, the stone that was meant to seal it had been rolled away. Turn the box lid over and show kids the picture of the angel.

An angel was at the tomb! Open your Bible to Matthew 28:5-6, and read: **"The angel said to the women, 'Do not be afraid, for I know that you are looking for Jesus, who was crucified. He is not here; he has risen, just as he said. Come and see the place where he lay.' "**

Notice what the angel said to the women: "Come and see the place where he lay." Come and see! Even the angels were so excited about Jesus' resurrection that they were inviting people to "come and see" for themselves. The women then hurried and invited more of Jesus' friends to come and see the empty tomb. Ask:

- **When have you been so surprised by something that you just had to tell someone?**
- **Have you ever seen something so amazing that you said to a friend or your parents, "Come and see!"?**
- **Who can you invite to church so that they can "come and see" about Jesus for themselves?**

Say: **You have a joyful job this week: I want you to invite one friend to "come and see" why we are rejoicing this Easter.**

Close in prayer: **Thank you, God, for the gift of Jesus. The empty tomb is such an amazing miracle. Help us share this wonderful news with people all around us.**

Then say: **When I count to three, I want you to say in a big voice: "Jesus is risen! Come and see!" Are you ready? One, two, three! Jesus is risen! Come and see!**

Because I Love You

Topic: Mother's Day

Scripture: Exodus 20:12

Simple Supplies: You'll need a Bible and a flower for each child.

Gather kids to the front, and give each one of them a flower. Say: **Today is Mother's Day. So, before we do anything else, let's honor our mothers. Go ahead and give your mom your flower, then come back to me! If your mom isn't here, you can save it for later or pick out another lady who is special to you and give her a flower.** Pause while kids do this, then ask:

- **How did you show honor to a mother right now?**
- **What other ways can we show honor to moms?**

Say: **We honored moms by giving them flowers. We can show honor by telling our moms we love them, by helping around the house, and by being pleasant to live with!** Mention other ways the children talked about.

Open your Bible to Exodus 20:12. Say: **This is what God has to say about our parents. "Honor your father and your mother, so that you may live long in the land the Lord your God is giving you."**

The Bible says to "honor" your mom. To honor means to show a deep respect and love for your mom. Sometimes she has to help you behave, but she does that because she loves you.

The next time your mom asks you to do something for her, remember to say cheerfully, "OK, Mom! I'll do it because I love you!" But be careful! You may surprise her so much that she faints! Then be ready to pick your mom up off the floor!

Ask the moms to stand, then say a prayer: **Dear God, we thank you so very much for all our mothers. We know that you want us to treat them in a loving and special way. Help us remember to do that all day every day, and not just on Mother's Day.**

Send the kids back, and tell them to hug their moms and tell them "Happy Mother's Day! I love you!"

Give It Up, Live It Up!

Topic: Memorial Day

Scripture: 1 John 2:2

Simple Supplies: You'll need a Bible, a flower, a flag, and a cross.

Say: **Memorial Day is a special day for remembering people who died in war defending our country. They sacrificed, or gave up, their lives so that we can live in a free country.**

I need two volunteers. Have a child stand up and hold the flower and another child stand up to hold the flag. **To remember the people who gave up their lives for us, we decorate their graves with flowers and flags. In fact, Memorial Day used to be called "Decoration Day," because people decorated the graves with flowers.** Ask:

• **Do you know anyone who died to defend our country?**

Say: **We thank God for the brave people who served to save our freedom.**

Now I need another volunteer, because I want to tell you about another symbol that reminds us of someone else who sacrificed his life for others. Have a child stand up and hold the cross.

Open your Bible to 1 John 2:2. Say: **Listen to this. The Bible says that "[Jesus] is the atoning sacrifice for our sins, and not only for ours but also for the sins of the whole world."**

Wow! Jesus gave up his life so that we can live forever with God. When we see a cross, we remember that Jesus gave up his life for us.

These symbols remind us of people who were willing to give up their lives so others might live. You, too, can help others. You can show kindness through your words and actions. You can share Jesus' love with others.

Walk behind each child who is holding an item, and pray: **Dear God, thank you for the people who gave their lives to serve our country. Thanks for flowers and flags and other reminders of** their bravery. Thanks for the cross that reminds us of Jesus who died so we all will live with you forever. In Jesus' name, amen.

Joy! Joy! Joy!

Topic: Father's Day

Scripture: Proverbs 10:1a

Simple Supplies: You'll need a Bible and mini Almond Joy candy bars.

Say: **I have a special treat for you today! But before I give you this yummy treat, I'd like you to treat all the dads here to a round of applause because today is Father's Day—a day we show honor to our dads. So dads, would you please stand up so we can honor you?** Let the dads stand. **Let's clap for our dads.** Let the children clap. **Thank you, dads!**

Open your Bible to Proverbs 10:1a, and say: **The Bible says, "A wise son [or daughter] brings joy to his [or her] father." You kids are a joy to be around, and I'll bet you are a joy to your dads! So here is a reminder of the joy you kids bring.** Pass out the Almond Joy candy bars, and encourage the children to eat the treats. Ask:

- **Sons and daughters, what can you do to bring some joy to your dad today?**
- **What can you do every day to let your dad know that you love him?**

Say: **Treat your dad special today. But remember to treat him special always. Doing nice things for your dad will make him happy, and it will also bring joy to God, who's your Father in heaven!**

Did you know that the tradition of celebrating fathers started in the church? In the early 1900s, Mrs. John B. Dodd wanted to

honor her own father, so she convinced her minister to salute fathers in a special church service. Hooray for Mrs. Dodd bringing joy to her father! It's neat that Father's Day started in the church.

Have all the fathers stand, and then close in prayer: **Dear God, thank you for our fathers. Help us show them how much we love them. Thank you that we have the most awesome Father of all—you! In the name of your Son, Jesus, amen.**

Say: **I have one more treat for you. The Bible says that a wise child brings joy to his father. Well, here's another Almond Joy candy bar—bring it to your dad! When you give this "little joy" to your dad today, be sure to tell him how much you love him and appreciate all he does for you!**

Freedom in Christ

Topic: Independence Day

Scripture: 2 Corinthians 3:17

Simple Supplies: You'll need a Bible and a flag.

Wave the flag, then say: **Since we're about to celebrate Independence Day here in America, we're going to talk about what it means to be free. If you're "independent" then you're free. But first, we're going to see what it feels like not to be free. Sit on your hands so you can't move them.**

Pause while kids do this.

Say: **What if I tell you to scratch your nose? Go ahead and try it. But don't move your hands!** Pause. **You can't scratch your nose easily, maybe with your shoulder! What if I tell you to pat your head?** Pause. **You can't pat your head, because your hands are trapped! You aren't free!** Ask:

• **What's it like to not be able to use your hands?**

After kids respond, let them "free" their hands. Let them scratch their noses now and then pat their heads. Ask:

- **How does it feel to have your hands free?**

Say: **Every July 4, the United States celebrates Independence Day. It's the anniversary of when we adopted the Declaration of Independence in 1776.**

Have kids sit on their hands. Say: **Before the Declaration, the people who lived here were ruled by another country across the ocean.** Ask the kids to wave their hands high without moving their hands from under them. **In 1776 the people said, "We're free!" They said, "We're independent. We're our own country."** Have the children move their hands and wave.

But did you know that if you believe in Jesus, you have an even better "Independence Day" to celebrate? Open your Bible to 2 Corinthians 3:17, and read: **"Now the Lord [Jesus] is the Spirit, and where the Spirit of the Lord is, there is freedom." When we ask Jesus to forgive the bad things we've done, Jesus forgives us! We're free! So when you see flags or fireworks or parades celebrating the United States' Independence Day, remember the best freedom you have: Where Jesus is, there is freedom!**

Ask kids to sit on their hands once more. Pray: **Dear God, please hear us as we silently tell you the bad things we've done.** Pause, then ask kids to "free" their hands and wave them high. **Thanks for the freedom of forgiveness. In Jesus' name, amen.**

Working for the King

Topic: Labor Day

Scripture: Colossians 3:23, 24b

Simple Supplies: You'll need a Bible and a toolbox filled with things people use when they work (such as a paintbrush, pencil, calculator, and spatula).

Say: **In America, Labor Day is a day that's set aside to honor everyone who works. I have some things that people use when they work. As I pull out each item, I want you to guess what type of worker would use that item.** Pull out each item, and let the children respond. **As I said, Labor Day is set aside to honor everyone who works, and this includes you!** Ask:

• **What chores do you have to do at home? at school?**

Say: **I don't know about you, but when I was little, my mom used to ask me to clean my room. Sometimes I'd push everything into the closet, under the bed, or in my drawers. Then I'd yell, "Done!" That wasn't the best way to clean my room, but it was fast.** Note: If you didn't clean your room as a child, substitute another chore you did.

Let's see what the Bible has to say about work.

Open your Bible to Colossians 3:23, 24b, then read: **"Whatever you do, work at it with all your heart, as working for the Lord, not for men...It is the Lord Christ you are serving."**

So even when you do your chores, you're not just working for your parents or your teacher, you're working for Jesus the king! Ask:

• **The next time you do chores, how can you remember that you're really working for Jesus?**

Say: **Here's a prayer that will help you remember that we work for Jesus. Leave one hand flat, and with your other hand make a fist to look like a hammer. The flat hand will remind us of Jesus' hands and how he died on the cross for us. The fist hand will** remind us of a hammer and that when we work, we are really serving Jesus.

Pray: **Dear God, thank you for sending Jesus to die for us so that we are free to live and work for you. Help us to remember that we work for you, the king! In Jesus' name we pray, amen.**

Election Day Twist

Topic: Election Day

Scripture: Titus 3:1

Simple Supplies: You'll need a Bible and two kinds of pretzels (straight and twisted) in bags.

Say: **Election Day is coming up, the day when we get the privilege of voting! I thought I'd let you vote right here, right now. However, you're not going to vote for a person, but for a pretzel! I have two kinds of pretzels.** Hold up one bag on your left and one on your right. **What pretzel do you think is best—the straight or the twisted? If you'd like to vote for this kind of pretzel, get up and stand on my left side. If you'd like to vote for this kind of pretzel, get up and stand on my right side.** Count the children on each side. If it's a tie, cast your own vote. Announce the winner.

Just like with real elections, you don't always get your first choice in every vote. I'm going to pass out the winning pretzel for you to munch on while I read what God has to say about people who are elected to rule over us. Pass out the winning pretzels.

Open your Bible to Titus 3:1. Say: **The Bible says, "Remind the people to be subject to rulers and authorities, to be obedient, to be ready to do whatever is good." When you're "subject" to someone, you have to obey him or her, and the Bible says to obey rulers and authorities—this includes the ones you didn't vote for.** Ask:

- **Who do you obey each day?**
- **Why does God want us to obey our leaders?**

Say: **God gives us parents and teachers to obey. We also have leaders who run our country who we need to obey. On Election Day, adults vote for the people who will run our cities and states and country. Let's say a prayer asking for God's blessings on our leaders. I'll say one thing and then when I point to you, you can say, "Bless them, Lord!" Are you ready?**

Dear God,

We pray for our leaders today.

"Bless them, Lord!"

Please help them in every way.

"Bless them, Lord!"

Be near them, dear Lord, we pray.

"Bless them, Lord!"

Please guide what they do and say.

"Bless them, Lord!"

In Jesus' name, amen.

No Greater Love

Topic: Veterans Day

Scripture: John 15:13

Simple Supplies: You'll need a Bible, markers, and one copy of the certificate (p. 252) for each veteran.

Ask:

- **Do you know anyone who has served in the armed forces—Navy, Army, Air Force, National Guard, or Marines, or Coast Guard?**
- **What do these people do to protect us?**

Say: **People who serve their country in these armed services are called veterans. They help guard our country and, if they have to, they fight to save our freedom. We honor these people on November 11. On November 11, 1918, the First World War ended. The day started out being called "Armistice Day" to help us remember the terrible effects of war and the hope for peace. In time, we also started to honor all people who serve to keep peace and freedom.**

Lay the certificates on the floor, and have the kids sign each one or draw a smiley face or cross on each one. While kids are doing this, say: **Today we're going to honor the people in our church who have served in the armed services to help protect us and our freedom.**

Open your Bible to John 15:13, and say: **Jesus told us about the ultimate sacrifice one can make for another: "Greater love has no one than this, that he lay down his life for his friends." There have been many men and women who've given their lives in support of their country by serving in the armed services. And there are many here today who have served selflessly in the armed services to help make sure each one of us has the freedom to worship God as we choose, to say and print what we believe, and to gather with the people we choose. How about we give the veterans here today a small token of our appreciation? But first, let's pray.**

God, we thank you for the veterans here with us today, and all those who have died or been injured in service to their country. Thanks for Jesus who gave his life so we all could live with you forever. In Jesus' name, amen.

Invite the veterans forward, and let the children give them the certificates.

Cute Quote! A pastor was serving in a rural parish in western Pennsylvania and was providing a children's message prior to Christmas. The pastor called the excited children forward, motioned toward all the Christmas decorations and the Christmas tree. He said, "This is a really special time of year. Does anyone know what season it is?"

A little boy waved his hand among the wriggling mass of children, saying, "I know! I know! It's hunting season!"

Veterans, We Appreciate You!

In recognition of the service you provided your country to keep peace and to keep freedom,

the children of _____ Church give you this certificate in appreciation

on the occasion of Veterans Day, _____.

"Greater love has no one than this, that he lay down his life for his friends." (John 15:13)

We Salute Your Bravery

Permission to photocopy this page from *The Humongous Book of Children's Messages* granted for local church use. Copyright © Group Publishing, Inc., P.O. Box 481, Loveland, CO 80539. www.grouppublishing.com

I Know Something You Don't Know

Topic: Christmas

Scripture: Luke 2:6-7

Simple Supplies: You'll need a Bible and a red poinsettia plant.

Say: **Look at this beautiful plant!** Ask:

- **Does anyone know what this plant is called?**
- **Where are the leaves? the stem? the flowers?**

Say: **This is a poinsettia plant. All your guesses about the leaves, stems, and flowers are great guesses. But actually, I know something you don't know! I'm going to tell you something that you can go home and tell your friends. Did you know that these tiny yellow things are actually the flowers and the bright red parts are the leaves?**

When I saw this poinsettia plant, it reminded me of Christmas and of Jesus. I'll tell you why in a minute. But first let's read about Jesus' birthday.

Mary and Joseph went to Joseph's hometown to take care of some business. And while they were there, Jesus was born. Open your Bible, and read Luke 2:6-7: **"While they were there, the time came for the baby to be born, and she gave birth to her first-born, a son. She wrapped him in cloths and placed him in a manger, because there was no room for them in the inn."**

Jesus is called the King of kings and the Lord of lords. God came to earth and his name is Jesus. But instead of coming in a fancy way, like we imagine kings, his birth was simple and tiny, kind of like these little flowers. Jesus, the

> **LEADER TIP**
>
> If a child does know about the poinsettia, say "Wow! [Name of child], you knew something many people don't know!" Then continue with the message.

> **LEADER TIP**
>
> Do not let children put any part of the poinsettia in their mouths.

King of kings and Lord of lords, spent his first night on earth in a manger—a smelly feeding trough for animals! What a simple, humble, tiny way to enter this world. Ask:

- What did you expect certain parts of the plant to be?
- How would you expect the King of kings to come to earth?

Say: **The poinsettia leaves, stems, and flowers were different from what we expected. Jesus coming as a baby, and being born in a stable, wasn't what people expected either. But God is a great God, and he is the God of the unexpected. Every time you see a poinsettia, remember Jesus the baby, who is the King of kings!**

Say a prayer: **Dear God, what a strange way to send your special Son, the King of kings and Lord of lords, to earth. A tiny helpless baby in a stable for animals. Thank you for sending him to save all of us. Help us as we tell others why this time of year is so special.**

Jesus Is Born

Topic: Christmas

Scripture: Matthew 2:1-12; Luke 2:1-20

Simple Supplies: You'll need a Bible and a large box filled with angel halos (sparkling garland) and robes for Mary, Joseph, the shepherds, and the wise men. On the outside of the box, write "Instant Christmas Pageant." Ask someone in the audience to bring a baby doll forward at the appropriate time.

Pretend you don't see the box when you begin your message. Say: **I love Christmas and being able to celebrate Jesus' birth, don't you? Let's hear some of the story.** Open your Bible, and read aloud Luke 2:1-7.

The story goes on to tell about the angels who sang, and the shepherds and the Magi who came to see Jesus. We sometimes call the Magi the wise men.

Wouldn't it be fun to see this story in action! Why don't you guys help me put on a Christmas pageant?

Look at the box, and look startled. **Well, what do you know! Here's a box of supplies just for us. It says "Instant Christmas Pageant." Let's dig into it and put on a show!**

Let's see, who wants to be a shepherd? Choose shepherds, and have them put on robes. Ask an adult helper or two to help with the costumes and positioning the actors on stage.

How about the wise guys? I mean the Magi who came from the east. Choose three kids, and costume and position them.

We need Joseph and Mary! Choose two kids, and costume and position them.

How 'bout them angels? Choose angels, and give them garland halos. If you have a manger, bring it out last and put it between Joseph and Mary.

Hmmm. Everything looks in place. But I have a feeling we're forgetting something. What are we forgetting? Wait for the kids to say "Jesus!" **Oh, my! We forgot baby Jesus.** Ask the person from the audience to bring the baby doll Jesus and either lay him in the manger or place him in "Mary's" arms.

Sing a song such as "Away in a Manger." Then gather the actors and actresses, and ask:

- **Who did we forget for a while in our Christmas pageant?**
- **How do people sometimes forget Jesus during Christmas?**

Say: **We almost forgot Jesus! Sometimes we get so busy with all the other fun things of Christmas that we forget the one who is right at the center of it all—Jesus! Let's always keep Jesus in the middle of our Christmas celebrations and activities. Jesus is what Christmas is all about!**

Let the kids take off their costumes and place them back in the box. As they do, have them say, "Thanks for being born to save us, Jesus."

LEADER TIP

If you have a manger, place it in the bottom of the box before filling it with costumes. If you have a shepherd's staff, place it in the box so it's sticking out partway. Ask one or two helpers to assist in getting out the costumes, dressing the characters, and positioning them. Mary and Joseph will be in the center, shepherds stand to one side, wise men at the other, and angels behind them.

Close by praying: **Dear Jesus, this time of year can get so busy and be so much fun that it is easy to forget that it is all about you. You are the best gift of all. We love you and want to remember you as we celebrate Christmas. In your name, amen.**

Scripture Index

New Testament

Topical Index